# Contents

**1** **Who are they? Write.**

> Gizmo   Hector Frost   Mike   Polly   Polly's mum   Smith   Queen of Ice Island

**1** Hector Frost

**2**

**3**

**4**

**5**

**6**

**7**

**2** **Look at Activity 1 and number.**

**a**   He's wearing boots and a hat. He likes football, adventures and dogs.   `4`

**b**   He's tall and thin. He's rich and he likes diamonds and dogs.

**c**   He likes driving a skidoo and he's strong.

**d**   She's beautiful and rich. She's got a diamond necklace.

**e**   She likes adventure and solving problems. She's got long black hair.

**f**   He's black and white. He's wearing a collar around his neck.

**g**   She's got a daughter and she likes to cook.

**3** Complete with the correct form of the verb.

1  At nine o'clock, she is _____ (play) football.

2  At eleven o'clock, she is _____ (have) a rest.

3  At twelve o'clock, she is _____ (eat) lunch.

4  At two o'clock, she is _____ (swim) in the lake.

5  At five o'clock, she is _____ (sleep).

**4** Put the words in order to make questions. Then look and write answers.

1  ( you / Do / swimming / lake / like / the / in / ? ) ✓

_____? _____.

2  ( like / Do / park / they / in / playing / the / ? ) ✓

_____? _____.

3  ( reading / she / Does / books / like / ? ) ✗

_____? _____.

**5** 🎧 Listen and match. Then answer the questions.

1  What's Mike doing?    He's studying. _____

2  What's Polly doing?    _____

3  What's Smith doing?    _____

**6** Look and write.

**1** She <u>rode on a bicycle</u> .

**2** They _____ with a ball.

**3** _____

**4** _____

**7** 🎧 1:10 Listen and match.

**8** Look at Activity 7 and write.

**1** She ____<u>listened</u>____ to music on Monday morning.

**2** He _____ English on Thursday morning.

**3** They _____ volleyball on Saturday afternoon.

**4** She _____ a football match on Wednesday evening.

**5** They _____ to the park on Sunday afternoon.

**6** He _____ the guitar on Tuesday evening.

**9** **Write the days.**

1   Yesterday was ___Monday___ . Today is Tuesday.

2   Today is Saturday. Tomorrow is _____.

3   Today is Thursday. Two days ago was _____.

4   Today is _____. Tomorrow is Wednesday.

5   It is Monday. In two days it's going to be _____.

6   Tomorrow is Sunday. Two days ago it was _____.

**10** **Write the correct years.**

Now it's 20 __ __. Two years ago it was 20 __ __. In four years it's going to be 20 __ __.

**11** **Listen and match. Then write.**

on Monday morning          two years ago          three days ago

two weeks ago          yesterday

1   She _____danced_____ at school _____.

2   He _____.

3   They _____.

4   She _____ that _____.

5   They _____.

# 1 Friends

## 1 Put the letters in order to make words.

Hair:

**1** (lndobe raih) _____

**3** (ladb) _____

**5** (yksip iarh) _____

**7** (kdra hria) _____

**9** (aighrtst riha) _____

**11** (ycurl hari) _____

Face:

**2** (etcu) _____

**4** (mdnaheos) _____

**6** (odgo-gkolnio) _____

**8** (auultibef) _____

**10** (souteachm) _____

**12** (edrab) _____

## 2 Look and complete the sentences. Use words from Activity 1.

**1**

I've got **blonde** hair.

**2**

I've got _____ hair.

**3**

I've got _____ hair.

**4**

I'm _____.

## 3 Write about yourself and your friends.

**1** I've got dark hair. _____

**2** _____

**3** _____

**4** _____

**4** Put the words in order to make questions and answers.

**1** does / look / what / she / like    <u>What does she look like</u> _____ ?

( hair / brown / curly )    <u>She's got curly brown hair</u> _____ .

**2** look / what / do / like / they    _____ ?

( hair / long / straight )    _____ .

**3** look / does / he / what / like    _____ ?

( face / thin / long )    _____ .

**5** Read and circle. Then tick (✓) the true sentences and cross (✗) the false sentences.

**1** He ( (is) / has got ) bald.    ✓

**2** He ( is / has got ) spiky hair.    ☐

**3** She ( has got / is ) long straight hair.    ☐

**4** She ( has got / is ) glasses.    ☐

**5** They ( are / have got ) tall.    ☐

**6** They ( are / have got ) short curly hair.    ☐

**6** Listen and complete.

| | Dad | Mum | Grandad |
|---|---|---|---|
| hair | bald | | |
| eyes | | | |
| other | | | |

**7** Complete the sentences about the people in Activity 6.

**1** Dad is bald. He has got _____ .

**2** Mum has got _____ .

**3** Grandad has got _____ .

**8** **Read and match.**

1   She has got a lot of friends because      **a**   he's very helpful and hard-working.

2   He hasn't got a lot of friends because      **b**   she's very shy.

3   She makes friends slowly because      **c**   she's friendly and kind.

4   He has got a lot of friends because      **d**   he's very bossy.

5   My friends say I'm not shy because      **e**   sporty!

6   My sister is lazy but      **f**   I'm too talkative!

**9** **What makes a good friend? Choose for you and tick (✓).**

# What makes a good friend?

| | | |
|---|---|---|
| **1** This person is friendly. | ✓ | **2** This person is shy. ☐ |
| **3** This person isn't kind. | ☐ | **4** This person isn't sporty. ☐ |
| **5** This person is clever. | ☐ | **6** This person is lazy. ☐ |
| **7** This person isn't talkative. | ☐ | **8** This person is helpful. ☐ |
| **9** This person is bossy. | ☐ | **10** This person is hard-working. ☐ |

**10** **Write sentences about five different people.**

bossy   kind   sporty   lazy   clever   shy
talkative   helpful   friendly   hard-working

1   My friend is _friendly and talkative_____.

2   My teacher is _____.

3   My _____.

4   _____.

5   _____.

**11** Listen and complete the sentences. 🎧 1:24

**1**  Peter

**2**  Katy

**3** 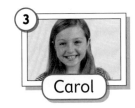 Carol

**4**  Tim

friendly   shy   talkative   bossy   sporty   talkative   helpful   hard-working

**1**   What's Peter like? He's _____ and _____.

**2**   What's _____? She's _____ but a little _____.

**3**   _____? She's _____ but she isn't _____.

**4**   _____? He's _____ and _____.

**12** Read and circle.

**1**   I like my new teacher ( (because) / but ) she's patient.

**2**   He's hard-working ( and / but ) clever.

**3**   My best friend is creative ( and / but ) very friendly. She's great!

**4**   She doesn't get good results ( because / but ) she's lazy.

**5**   He's lazy at home ( but / and ) he's hard-working in class.

**6**   She's clever ( because / but ) very bossy. I don't like her.

**13** 🎧 1:25 Listen and match.

**1**   Sally           **2**   Jane's grandparents           **3**   Tony           **4**   Lisa

   talkative              shy              helpful              kind

**14** Think about two friends. Write sentences to explain why you like them.

My best friend is helpful but talkative. I like her because she is friendly.

_____

_____

**1**

## 15 Read. Then number the pictures in order.

a
Has he got a beard?
I don't know.

b
Oh, no, I can't see the skidoo now.
Let's go inside.

c
What do the thieves look like?

d
Why is Gizmo barking?
WOOF!

e
It's the driver of the skidoo!
He's bald! Follow him!

f
I like Gizmo because he's very clever and helpful.

## 16 Look at Activity 15 and tick (✓).

**1** Who are Mike and Polly following?

a      b      c

**2** Where is Gizmo waiting?

a      b      c

## 17 Read the definitions and write the words.

**1** we can use this to travel on the snow     skidoo

**2** the hair growing on a man's face     _____

**3** the noise a dog makes     _____

**4** to walk behind someone     _____

**18** Read, think and write 1 to 5 (1 = not important, 5 = very important). Then compare with a partner.

Help your friends.

| How can you help? | You | Your friend |
|---|---|---|
| **1** Listen when your friends speak. | | |
| **2** Share your things. | | |
| **3** Be friendly. | | |
| **4** Invite others to work with you. | | |
| **5** Offer: 'Can I help you?' | | |

Listen when your friends speak. 5.

Share your things. 4.

## PHONICS & SPELLING

**19** Add *–er* or *–or* to make new words.

**1** invent     <u>inventor</u>     **2** act     _____

**3** collect     _____     **4** direct     _____

**5** view     _____     **6** tall     _____

**20** Write sentences with each of the new words from Activity 19.

<u>My mum is an inventor.</u>

_____

_____

_____

**21** **Circle the odd word out.**

| **1** | self-portrait | art gallery | paintings | (surprised) |
|---|---|---|---|---|
| **2** | abstract | happy | expressionism | post-impressionism |
| **3** | etching | painting | expressionism | self-portrait |
| **4** | warm | soft | cool | detail |
| **5** | abstract | sharp | impressionism | expressionism |

**22** **Look, think and write.**

abstract    post-impressionism    expressionism

**1**     **2**     **3**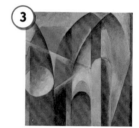

__post-impressionism__    _____    _____

**23** **Read and circle.**

This is a self-portrait of me. I like it because it has got lots of ¹ ( detail / etching ). I can see very small things, like the hairs of my beard. This is called an ² ( portrait / etching ) because there is no colour in it. My favourite style of art is ³ ( abstract / expressionism ) because I like the bright colours and the ⁴ ( sharp / soft ) lines. I don't like the soft colours of ⁵ ( post-impressionism / expressionism ).

**24** **What do you like about art? Complete the sentences.**

My favourite type of art is _____.

I like it because _____.

# Wider World

**25** Look, read and match.

a

Chris

**1**
- no brothers or sisters
- small
- quiet
- a lot of friends
- grandparents take care of me
- very happy together

**2**
- big family
- two brothers
- argue sometimes
- talk about our problems
- love each other a lot
- happy together

b

Lim

**26** Look at Activity 25 and complete the paragraph.

She/He lives with _____

He/She has a _____ family. He/She has _____ brothers/sisters.

_____

_____

_____

_____

**27** Write answers for you.

**1**   Is your family big or small? _____

**2**   Have you got any brothers or sisters? _____

**3**   Do your grandparents look after you? _____

**4**   Do you talk about your problems with your family? _____

**28** **You are writing an email to your mum about a family you are staying with. Tick the things you will write about.**

☐ your favourite hobbies

☐ the names of the family members

☐ what the family member look like

☐ the family's house

☐ what jobs the parents do

☐ what the family members are like

☐ if you are enjoying yourself or not

☐ what time you go to bed.

**29** **Imagine you are staying with this family in London. Complete the email.**

From: _____

To: _____

Subject: My stay in London

Hi _____,

I'm having a _____ time here in London.

Emily is _____.

She's got _____.

She is _____ and _____.

I like her because _____.

Steven is _____.

He's got _____.

He's _____ and _____ but _____

_____.

Their mum is _____.

She's got _____.

She's _____ and _____.

See you soon.

Love, _____

Emily    Steven

**30** **Read and match.**

bald   beautiful   clever   cute   sporty

**1**   good-looking for a baby or young animal _____

**2**   likes games like football and volleyball _____

**3**   good at thinking up new ideas _____

**4**   good-looking (for women) _____

**5**   no hair _____

**31** **Listen and complete.**

bossy   spiky   sporty   talkative   dark   because

My friend's name is Miki. She's tall and she's got [1]_____, [2]_____ hair. She's got brown eyes and she wears glasses. She likes skirts and colourful t-shirts.

She's very [3]_____. She loves basketball! She's a bit [4]_____, but it's OK. I like her [5]_____ she's [6]_____ and she makes me laugh.

**32** **Think about a friend. Answer the questions.**

What does he/she look like? _____

_____

What's he/she like? _____

_____

**I CAN**

I can ask and answer about what someone looks like.

I can talk about what someone is like.

I can write a friendly email.

# 2 My life

**1** Read and match.

**1** the rubbish    **2** my teeth    **3** notes in class    **4** my face

**5** to bed early    **6** my bed    **7** on time    **8** my room

**9** for a test    **10** my homework

**a** wash ☐    **b** brush ☐    **c** make ☐    **d** tidy ☐

**e** take ☐    **f** go ☐    **g** do ☐    **h** be ☐

**i** take out 1    **j** revise ☐

**2** 🎧 1:35 Look and complete. Then listen and tick (✓) or cross (✗) for Dan.

| | | | Dan |
|---|---|---|---|
| **1** | | I _____brush my teeth_____ in the morning. | |
| **2** | | I _____ every day. | |
| **3** | | I _____ every day. | |
| **4** | | I _____ for school every day. | |
| **5** | | I _____ in class. | |
| **6** | | I _____ for a test. | |
| **7** | | I _____ early. | |
| **8** | | I _____ every day. | |

**3** 🎧 **Listen and match.**

| | | | |
|---|---|---|---|
| **1** | Tim and Kelly | **a** | brush his teeth |
| **2** | Kelly | **b** | take out the rubbish |
| **3** | Tim | **c** | say good night to their parents |
| **4** | Dad | **d** | revise for a test |
| **5** | Mum | **e** | go to bed early |
| **6** | Helen | **f** | tidy his room |
| **7** | Paul | **g** | wash her face |

**4** 🎧 **Look at Activity 3. Make sentences using *should* and *must*. Then listen to check.**

**1**  Tim and Kelly should say good night to their parents.

**2**  _____

**3**  _____

**4**  _____

**5**  _____

**6**  _____

**7**  _____

**5** **Write sentences about what you and your family *should* and *must* do before bed.**

**1**  I should _____.

**2**  My _____ should _____.

**3**  I must _____.

**4**  My _____ must _____.

**6**   **Read and complete. Then listen and check.**

never   usually   often   always   sometimes

I ¹_____ get up at seven o'clock.

I should leave home at eight fifteen.

I should walk to school but I ²_____ have to run! I am ³_____ on time.

School starts at eight forty-five but I should be there at eight thirty. ⁴ _____ I get into trouble with my teacher.

Today I must revise for my weekly test. It's tomorrow. I've got my school books, but I ⁵ _____ forget to take notes in class. I must remember today!

5 days ⎤
4 days ⎤
3 days ⎤
2 days ⎤
1 day ⎤
0 days ⎤

| | get up at 7.00 a.m. |
| | run to school |
| | be on time |
| | get in trouble with my teacher |
| | forget to take notes |

**7**  **Listen and tick (✓). Then write.**

| MY WEEK | | | | | |
|---|---|---|---|---|---|
| | Monday | Tuesday | Wednesday | Thursday | Friday |
| **1** brush my teeth | ✓ | | | | |
| **2** make my bed | | | | | |
| **3** do my homework | | | | | |
| **4** take out the rubbish | | | | | |

1   <u>She always brushes her teeth.</u>

2   _____

3   _____ in the evenings.

4   _____

**8** **Read. Then number the sentences in the correct order.**

Saturday morning

☐ Finally, I do my homework.

☐ First, I get up early and get dressed.

☐ Then I tidy my room.

☐ Next, I help make breakfast.

**9** **Read and complete.**

( finally   first   then   next )

Every Monday is the same. ¹ _____, I get up and make my bed. ² _____ I brush my teeth and get ready for school. ³ _____, I eat my breakfast and do my homework. I always do my homework on time. ⁴ _____, I take out the rubbish and ride to school on my bicycle.

**10** **Write a paragraph about Dina's schedule.**

( finally   first   then   next )

7.15 a.m.   make my bed

8.15 a.m.   pack lunch and wash up

12.00 p.m. help on farm

4.00 p.m. hot shower and relax

First, Dina _____

_____

_____

_____

**11** Read. The number the pictures in order.

**12** Look and write sentences.

room   bed   dinner   ~~lunch~~   dog   TV

He eats lunch at
half past twelve.

**13** Think about your day. Then write sentences.

At seven o'clock I _____. At eight o'clock I _____.

_____

**14** When should you say *thank you*? Tick (✓) or cross (✗).

Always say
'Thank you'.

**1**

your friend doesn't want to help

**2**

someone looks after you when you are unwell

**3** you give flowers

**4**

HAPPY BIRTHDAY HAVE A GREAT DAY!

you get a birthday card

**15** Listen and complete the sentences.

PHONICS & SPELLING

teaches   writes   catches   sees   studies   reads

**1** She often _____ her friend after school.

**2** He _____ about Poland in the school library.

**3** She _____ Maths to my sister.

**4** Emma _____ her notes for the test.

**5** He always _____ emails to me.

**6** The dog _____ the ball.

**16** What is the third person singular for each verb? Write in the correct column.

smile   pick   hop   cross   miss   wait   wash   rain   understand

| /s/ | /z/ | /iz/ |
|-----|-----|------|
|     |     |      |
|     |     |      |
|     |     |      |

**17** **Read and complete.**

nutrients   stomach   saliva   tongue   pancreas

Our digestive system starts as soon as we smell food. First, your mouth produces
¹____saliva____. Then your ²_____ tastes the food. Next, the food
travels down to the ³_____. Here it is broken down.

Then your ⁴_____helps your body absorb proteins and
⁵_____from the food in your small intestine.

**18** **Look at Activity 17. Write the parts of your body that help you to …**

**1**   chew food _____

**2**   taste food _____

**3**   break down food _____

**4**   absorb proteins and nutrients _____

**19** **Read. Then number the sentences in the correct order.**

**a**   Digestion starts when you smell food.   `1`   nose

**b**   Your colon absorbs water and minerals.   mouth

**c**   Your stomach stores food and breaks it down.

**d**   Saliva makes food easy to swallow.

**e**   The small intestine gets help from the pancreas
     and liver to absorb proteins and nutrients.

stomach

small
intestine

colon

# Wider World

**20** Look and complete.

> ~~always~~   always eats   his   must get up   often eat
> should   sometimes sings   usually get up

I don't like mornings. My big brother ¹_____always_____ gets up at five

o'clock. He ²_____ early every day because he's a farmer.

He ³_____ songs in the morning. ⁴_____ songs are

horrible. I can't sleep after that. I ⁵_____ at six o'clock because

I'm hungry. I like eggs for breakfast but I ⁶_____ toast. Why?

Because my brother ⁷_____ all of our eggs at 5.30 a.m.

He ⁸_____ give me some but he doesn't. Grrr!

**21** Read and find six more differences. Then correct the paragraph.

```
7.00 a.m. – get up, wash face, have milk and cheese for breakfast
8.30 a.m. – walk to school with friends
12.30 p.m. – go home for lunch, usually have soup or meatballs
1.15 p.m. – go back to school
3.00 p.m. – school finishes, go to music or art lessons
5.00 p.m. – see friends at park and play football
7.30 p.m. – have dinner
8.00 p.m. – do homework, watch TV
10.00 p.m. – have a shower, go to bed
```

                                                             has

Tarek Aktas lives in Ankara, Turkey. He gets up at seven o'clock and ~~cooks~~ breakfast. Then

he walks to school with his sister. He has lunch at school at half past twelve. He has soup

or meatballs. At two o'clock, school finishes and he goes to music or art lessons. At five

o'clock, he sees his friends at the park and plays volleyball. He does his homework and

watches TV, then he has dinner.  He has a shower and then he goes to bed at nine o'clock.

**22** Read. Then number the paragraphs in the correct order.

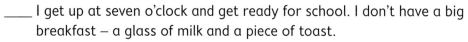

___ I get up at seven o'clock and get ready for school. I don't have a big breakfast – a glass of milk and a piece of toast.

_1_ Hi! My name's Nikos and I'm from Patras, Greece. My week is great because I play every day!

___ School finishes at half past one. I go home and have lunch. Then I do all my homework or revise for a test.

___ I get home at about half past seven and have a shower and eat dinner. I usually go to bed at half past ten, but sometimes it's later.

___ At eight o'clock, I walk to school with my friends, Andreas and Angelo. We talk about sports or the latest video games.

___ Next, I go to the sports centre and play basketball with my team. We are really good.

**WRITING TIP!**

We use *and* and *but* to join two ideas.
*and* = similar ideas
*I get up at six o'clock and go to the pool.*
*but* = contrasting ideas
*I usually stay at home, but sometimes I visit friends.*

**23** Look at Penny's diary. Write a short paragraph about her day.

| MONDAY | TUESDAY | WEDNESDAY | THURSDAY | FRIDAY |
|---|---|---|---|---|
| 7.30 a.m. have breakfast | 7.30 a.m. have breakfast | 7.30 a.m. have breakfast | 7.30 a.m. have breakfast | 7.30 a.m. have breakfast |
| 8.00 a.m. go to school | 8.00 a.m. go to school | 8.00 a.m. go to school | 8.00 a.m. go to school | 8.00 a.m. go to school |
| 4.00 p.m. come home | 4.00 p.m. come home | 4.00 p.m. come home | 4.00 p.m. come home | 4.00 p.m. come home |
| 5.30 p.m. music - piano | 5.00 p.m. English lessons | 5.30 p.m. swimming | 5.00 p.m. English lessons | 6.00 p.m. help in our shop |

Penny always has breakfast at half past seven. _____

On Mondays, Penny has _____

_____

_____.

**24** **Read and match.**

> be on time    brush my teeth    homework
> revise for a test    take notes    wash my face

**1**    use a toothbrush and toothpaste

_____

**2**    listen and write

_____

**3**    schoolwork to do after school finishes

_____

**4**    we must do this a lot to get 100%

_____

**5**    not early and not late

_____

**6**    use water and soap

_____

**25** **Put the words in order to make sentences. Then match.**

**1**    day / every / must / you / make / your / bed

_____

**2**    the / in / brush / morning / teeth / should / they / their

_____

**3**    help / the / parents / should / we / our / tidy / house

_____

**4**    this / 10.00 p.m. / homework / must / I / finish / before

_____

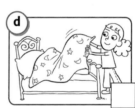

**26**    **Read and complete. Then listen and check.**

I ¹ ... do my homework every night. Then I help my dad take the rubbish out and ² ... the kitchen. ³ ... , I email friends or play on my computer. ⁴ ... , I go to bed. I usually go to bed at 10.00 p.m., but ⁵ ... I'm late. I never go to bed early!

> tidy
> sometimes
> always
> finally
> next

 **I CAN**

I can give orders and advice using **you must** and **you should**.

I can use sequence adverbs **first**, **next**, **then** and **finally**.

I can write a short description of daily activities.

# 3 Free time

## 1 Look and match. Then draw the missing picture.

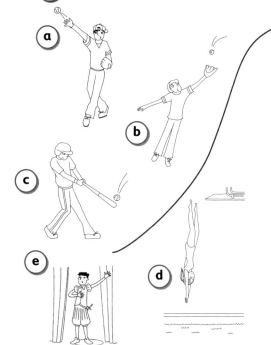

1 acting

2 throwing

3 hitting

4 catching

5 diving

6 kicking

7 telling jokes

8 reading poetry

9 playing computer games

10 doing puzzles

## 2 Look and write. Use the words from Activity 1.

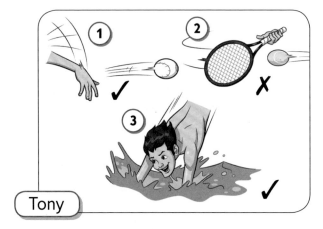

Tony

Bill

1  I like _____throwing_____.

3  I like _____.

5  I _____.

2  I don't like _____.

4  I _____.

6  I _____.

## 3  Listen. Look at Activity 2. Who is talking – Tony or Bill?

**4** Look and complete.

is   they're   I'm   at   isn't   jumping   good   ~~what~~

**1**
1 _What_ are you good at?

2 _____ good 3 _____ throwing.

**4**
7 _____ good at running and 8 _____.

**3**
What 5 _____ they 6 _____ at?

**2**
He 4 _____ good at catching.

**5** Look and write sentences.

1 ✓  ✗    _Molly isn't_ _____

_____

2  ✓ ✗    _____

_____

Molly

Felix

**6** What are your friends good at? What aren't they good at? Write sentences.

1   ✓   _____

2   ✗   _____

**7** **Make a wordsearch. Then swap with a partner.**

> trampolining    playing chess    drawing    playing the drums
> running races    rollerblading    making models
> singing karaoke    skateboarding    writing stories

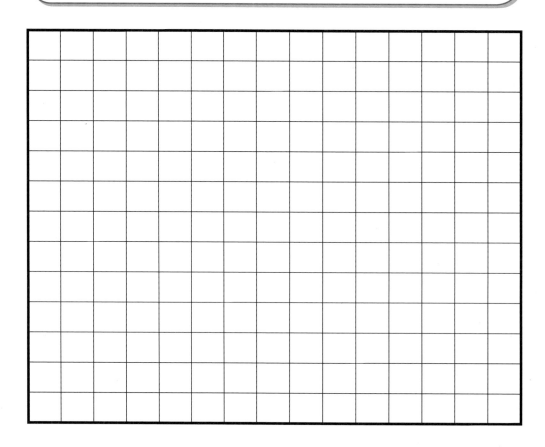

**8** **Look and write.** 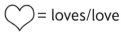 = is/are good at    = loves/love    = doesn't/don't like

**1**   _____

**2**   _____

**3**   _____

**4**   _____

**5** _____

**9** Read and complete.

| YESTERDAY | Ellis | Jasmin | Maddy and Arlo |
|---|---|---|---|
| 7.00 a.m. | sleeping | eating breakfast | walking to school |
| 11.00 a.m. | studying music | writing a story | swimming |
| 12.00 a.m. | eating lunch | eating lunch | playing with friends |
| 2.45 p.m. | having computer class | drawing in class | reading in English class |
| 5.00 p.m. | playing football at school | doing a project | eating ice cream with friends |
| 8.00 p.m. | singing in the bath | meeting friends | watching TV |

**1** What was Ellis doing yesterday at 7.00 a.m.? He was _____.

**2** What _____ Maddy and Arlo doing yesterday at 11.00 a.m.?

They were _____.

**3** What _____ Jasmin doing yesterday at 12.00 a.m.?

She _____ lunch.

**4** What _____ Maddy and Arlo doing yesterday at 2.45 p.m.?

They _____ in English class.

**5** What _____ Ellis _____ yesterday at _____?

_____ football at school.

**6** What _____ Jasmin _____ yesterday at 8.00 p.m.?

_____

**10** Read and complete. Then look at Activity 9 and circle the correct answer.

**1** Was Jasmin eating breakfast at 7.00 a.m.? ( Yes, she _____. / No, she wasn't. )

**2** _____ Maddy and Arlo _____ lunch at 12.00 a.m.?

( Yes, they _____. / No, they _____. )

**3** _____ Ellis _____ a project at 2.45 p.m.?

( Yes, he was. / No, _____. )

**4** _____ Maddy and Arlo _____ TV at 8.00 p.m.?

( Yes, _____. / No, _____. )

**11** Read. Then number the pictures in order.

**12** Read and circle.

**1**    Polly's mum is good at ( telling jokes / cooking / catching ).

**2**    Mike plays chess every ( Tuesday / Sunday / Saturday ).

**3**    Polly wants to ( cook dinner / find the thieves / tidy her room ).

**4**    Mike and Polly see ( a cat / some food / the skidoo ).

**5**    Mike and Polly ( are / isn't / aren't ) good at finding thieves.

**13** Write answers.

**1**    What is Mike good at? _____

**2**    When does Mike do his hobby? _____

**3**    Where was the skidoo going? _____

**4**    Who was cooking? _____

**5**    What was Polly doing at 2.00 a.m. on Thursday? _____

**14** Put the words in order to make sentences. Then match.

1 good / and / at / acting / I'm / singing

_____

2 like / we / drawing / and / making / things

_____
_____

3 at / hitting / very / I'm / catching / good / and

_____
_____

**a** they / take / art classes / should

_____
_____

**b** a sports team / should / join / she

_____
_____

**c** go to / a drama club / she / should

_____
_____

**PHONICS & SPELLING**

**15**  **Listen and circle.**

1 Is it fun to climb a mountain? ⬈ ⬊

2 Yes, it is. ⬈ ⬊

3 She plays football. ⬈ ⬊

4 Are they having a picnic? ⬈ ⬊

5 No, they aren't. ⬈ ⬊

6 Is he good at computer games? ⬈ ⬊

**16** **Read and complete. Then circle.**

at   like   computer   throwing

1 Do you _____ football? ⬈ ⬊

2 He is good _____ running. ⬈ ⬊

3 Is Dan playing on the _____? ⬈ ⬊

4 They are _____ balls. ⬈ ⬊

**Lesson 6**

**17** Put the letters in order to make words. Then complete the sentences.

ICT

sppa _____       oadupl _____

dwonoald _____       nolnie _____

ciaosl demia _____

**1**  You can _____ music, films and books from the internet to your phone.

**2**  These cooking _____ teach you how to cook.

**3**  YouTube and Facebook are _____ sites.

**4**  I found out information about the new app _____.

**5**  You can _____ photos to your favourite site.

**18** What can these hobby apps do? Read and complete.

learn to concentrate     make a photo poster
online competitions     upload to social media

**Chess Mover**

★ learn new moves
★ (1) _____
★ play with people all over the world
★ keeps score
★ (2) _____

**Photo Cut**

★ make photos smaller / bigger
★ (3) _____
★ print high quality photos
★ (4) _____
★ learn about lighting

**19** Write about an app that you like to use.

- What is it for?
- What does it do?
- What can you do with it?

_____

_____

_____

# Wider World

**20** **Read and complete.**

> broom   flying   running   seven

Are you good at ¹_____ with a broom? Are you good at catching? Well, quidditch is for you! You too can now play Harry Potter's exciting sport – but there's no ²_____.

Quidditch has rules from rugby, dodgeball and handball. Each team has ³_____ players. There's one keeper, two beaters, one seeker and three chasers.

The keeper guards the goal posts. The seeker and the chasers chase the snitch. The snitch is a fast runner. A team wins 30 points when they catch him.

Everyone has a ⁴_____ between their legs. They play the game with volleyballs and dodgeballs.

**21** **Read the text in Activity 20 again. Then answer the questions.**

**1**   What two things should you be good at to play quidditch? _____

**2**   Can you fly in this game? _____

**3**   Is the snitch a person? _____

**22** **Think of a sport you like. Complete the sentences.**

> • What is it called?
> • What must you be good at?
> • How do you play it?

The sport is called _____.

You must be good at _____.

To play you must _____

_____.

**23** **Read and match.**

**1**

Hi Grandma! 🖤

Can you help me with my cooking classes? I know you're good at cooking.

I can catch the bus at 10.00 a.m. Can Grandad help me with my art project? He's good at drawing and painting.

Love, Hayley.

**a**

I want to start acting – thank you for telling me!

Thursday afternoon is good for me.

See you later.

**2**

Hey, Pete! What time do you want to meet at the park? There's skateboarding and trampolining there.

Call me later. ☺ Danny

**b**

Yes, of course I can help you.

Maybe you can sleep over as well.

Yes, he can. Bring your pencils and paints, too.

See you on Saturday morning.

**3**

Hello Rina,

We can try singing karaoke, playing the piano, acting or dancing at the new youth centre. Which one do you want to do?

Let's walk there at four o'clock. It's open on Wednesday and Thursday afternoons.

When do you want to go?

Talk later, Jane.

**c**

Sounds good! I can meet at 10.00 a.m. on Saturday.

OK, speak later!

**24** **Imagine you want a friend to try a new hobby with you. Write your text message. Then write their response.**

**WRITING TIP!**

We use emojis and symbols in messages to communicate feelings and ideas. What do you think these pictures show?

_____

_____

_____

_____

**25** **Match.**

| diving | joke | karaoke | trampolining | computer game | writing stories |

**1** a jumping sport

_____

**2** reading and singing along to music

_____

**3** something you can play on a TV

_____

**4** jumping fingers first into a swimming pool _____

**5** this should be funny

_____

**6** we can do this with a pen and paper

_____

**26** **Look and write.**

🏆 = is/are good at      ✗ = isn't good at

**1** Sam 🏆 _____

**2** Anna ✗ _____

**3** The children 🏆 _____

**27** **Write the missing word. Then write the answer.**

**1** What _____ she doing yesterday?

_____

**2** _____ they _____ races?

_____

**28** **Complete the sentences for you.**

I'm good at _____.

My hobby is _____.

**I CAN**

I can talk about what people are good at and are not good at doing.

I can talk about what people were doing yesterday.

I can write a simple text message making an arrangement.

# 4 Around the world

**1** 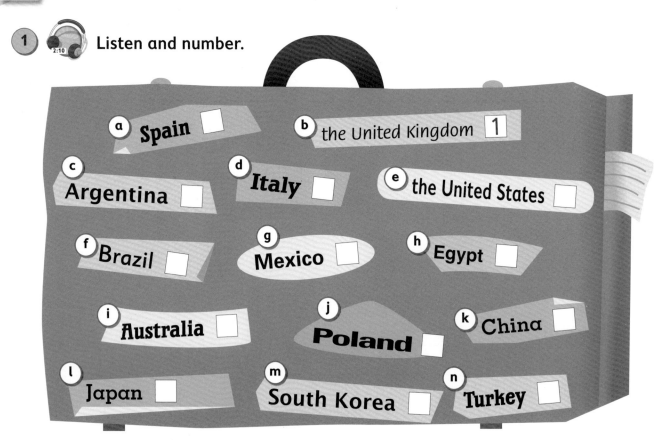 Listen and number.

a Spain ☐    b the United Kingdom ☐ 1

c Argentina ☐    d Italy ☐    e the United States ☐

f Brazil ☐    g Mexico ☐    h Egypt ☐

i Australia ☐    j Poland ☐    k China ☐

l Japan ☐    m South Korea ☐    n Turkey ☐

**2** Complete the crossword. Use words from Activity 1.

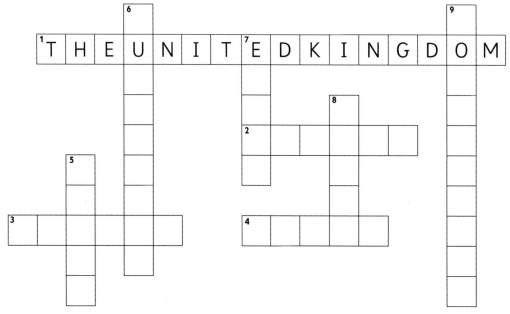

¹T H E U N I T E D K I N G D O M

## 3 Look and write.

1 <u>There's</u> an old man under _____.

2 _____ two birds _____ umbrella.

3 _____ an umbrella on _____.

4 _____ cats on the _____.

5 _____ monkeys in the sea.

## 4 Read and write *a*, *some* or *any*.

1 There are __<u>some</u>__ long rivers in the United States.

2 There isn't _____ rainforest in Italy.

3 There aren't _____ giraffes in the United Kingdom.

4 There are _____ old houses in Spain.

5 There are _____ big waterfalls in Brazil and Argentina.

## 5 Read and write.

1 hippos / China / ✗    <u>There aren't any hippos in China.</u>

2 a rainforest / Australia / ✓    _____

3 a snowy mountain / Egypt / ✗    _____

4 elephants / Mexico / ✗    _____

5 beautiful beaches / Spain / ✓    _____

## 6 Write three sentences about your country.

1 _____

2 _____

3 _____

**7** **Look and complete.**

| | | the United Kingdom | Spain |
|---|---|---|---|
| 1 | <u>volcano</u> es | ✗ | ✓ |
| 2 | a _____ | ✓ | ✓ |
| 3 | _____ s | ✓ | ✓ |
| 4 | _____ s | ✗ | ✗ |
| 5 | _____ s | ✓ | ✓ |
| 6 | a _____ | ✓ | ✓ |
| 7 | _____ s | ✗ | ✓ |
| 8 | a _____ | ✓ | ✓ |

**8** **Look at Activity 7 and complete the sentences. Write three more sentences.**

**1** In the United Kingdom and Spain there are some ___<u>statues</u>___.

**2** In Spain there are some _____ but in the United Kingdom there aren't _____.

**3** In the United Kingdom and Spain there is a _____.

**4** _____

**5** _____

**6** _____

**9** Look at Activity 7 again. Complete the sentences.

1 _____ pyramids in Spain?

No, there aren't.

2 _____ lakes in Spain?

_____

3 _____ volcanoes in the United Kingdom?

_____

4 _____ caves in the United Kingdom?

_____

**10** Read, guess and write. Then listen and tick (✓) your correct answers.

1 Are there any beaches in Australia?     Yes, there are. ☐

2 Is there a rainforest in Brazil? _____ ☐

3 Are there any volcanoes in Japan? _____ ☐

4 Are there any volcanoes in Mexico? _____ ☐

5 Is there a mountain taller than 5,000 metres in Spain? _____ ☐

6 Is there a river longer than the Amazon in China? _____ ☐

**11** Write your own quiz.

1 Are there any pyramids in Argentina?

No, there aren't.

2 _____

_____

3 _____

_____

**12** Write. Then number the pictures in order.

> Are there any roads to Bollington Hall?  Where are the tracks going?
> Yes, there are.  WHAT? Stop the kids!
> The tracks are going to Bollington Hall!  They can't have the diamonds!

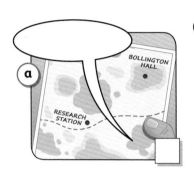

_____

_____

_____

_____

_____

_____

**13** Write correct sentences about the story in Activity 12.

**1** Hector Frost has got a map.

<u>Mike and Polly have got a map.</u>

**2** There aren't any roads to the research station.

_____

**3** There are some tracks going towards town.

_____

**4** Frost is happy to see the kids in the forest.

_____

**14** Read and choose two teams for an English project. Team members should be good at different things.

I can draw.

Peter

I'm good at using computers and the internet.

I'm good at writing.

I love reading and writing.

Sofia

I like finding things on the internet.

Sandra

I'm good at painting.

Diego

Maria

George

| Skill | Writing | Art | Computers |
|---|---|---|---|
| Team A | Sandra | _____ | _____ |
| Team B | _____ | _____ | _____ |

**15**  Listen and complete the sentences.

**PHONICS & SPELLING**

1 She _____ isn't _____ working today.

2 Please _____ wait for me.

3 He _____ shopping in the market.

4 She _____ want tea.

5 We _____ helped them.

6 I _____ enjoy the trip.

**16** Read and circle the contraction.

1 I don't like travelling by train.

2 He doesn't shop in other cities.

3 We didn't cook anything in our hotel.

4 We weren't visiting a desert.

**17** **Read and circle.**

Our Solar System is a fascinating place. Earth ¹( (is)/ are ) part of our Solar System. There ²( are / aren't  nine ) ³( moons / planets ) in the Solar System, which move around the Sun.

Our planet, Earth, has the best environment for life. There is a lot of ⁴( gravity / air ), water and land for animals and plants to live. Earth has ⁵( gravity  / air ), which keeps us on the ground. The earth has got five oceans and one ⁶( moon / planet ). There aren't any ⁷( rings / moons ) around Earth.

Mars is also very interesting. There ⁸( are / is ) a lot of mountains and hills on Mars. There aren't ⁹( some / any ) volcanoes. There are two moons. Like Earth, it has got a lot of land. Mars had water in the past.

**18** **Write about an imaginary planet.**

- What is your planet called?
- How many moons has it got?
- How many volcanoes and lakes are there?
- How much land and water is there?
- What is the environment like on your planet?
- Who lives on your planet?

My planet is called _____

My planet has got _____ moons. _____

There are _____ volcanoes and _____.

There is _____ land and _____ water.

The environment is _____.

_____ live(s) on this planet.

# Wider World

**19** Put the words in order to make words.

**1** stefor _____

**2** mapteeret _____

**3** balore _____

**4** caliport _____

**20** Match the kinds of forests to the descriptions.

tropical   temperate   boreal

**1**
_____
- cold climates
- long winters, short summer
- a lot of snow

**2**
_____
- large and wet
- birds and gorillas live here
- very warm

**3**
_____
- rain and snow
- foxes and rabbits live here

**21** Why are forests important? Write sentences, giving three reasons.

Forests are important because _____

_____

_____

_____ .

**22**  **Listen and circle.**

1 Catherine is talking to her ( (grandma)/ grandad ).

2 Catherine is in ( Brazil / Mexico ).

3 Catherine is in a ( tropical forest / city ).

4 There are some ( beaches / pyramids ) in Rio de Janeiro.

5 There's a big ( volcano / statue ).

**23** **Complete the postcard.** | animals   beautiful   ~~Grandad~~   rainforest   lakes   trees

Dear ¹ __Grandad__ ,

Hello!  I'm in the Amazon ² _____ in Brazil!
It's very ³ _____ here. There are some very
tall green ⁴ _____ in the rainforest and some
scary ⁵ _____ , too! There aren't any
⁶ _____ but there is a big river!

See you soon!

Catherine

POSTAL SYSTEM
SEP 12

**WRITING TIP!**

Adjectives go before nouns, e.g.
*There's a big statue.*
Adjectives go after the verb *be*, e.g.
*It's very old.*

**24** **Imagine you are on holiday. Write a postcard to a friend.**

Hi _____ ,

I'm in _____ .

It's _____ here. There are some _____

_____ .

There aren't any _____

_____ .

See you _____ ! _____

**25** **Read and match.**

> Argentina   a volcano   city   pyramids
> rainforest   South Korea   the United States

**1** there are some famous ones in Egypt

_____

**2** a country in South America

_____

**3** this is an area with lots of trees that has lots of wet weather _____

**4** a country in North America

_____

**5** this is bigger than a town

_____

**6** hot liquid sometimes comes out of this type of mountain _____

**7** a country in Asia _____

**26** **Put the words in order to make questions. Then write the answers.**

**1** there / is / desert / in / Australia / a   (✓)

<u>Is there a desert in Australia?</u> _____

**2** is / rainforest / there / a / Italy / in   (✗)

_____

**3** are / statues / in / Brazil / there / any   (✓)

_____

**27** 2:28   **Listen and complete.**

Last year I went on holiday with my family. We went to ¹_____ and visited some ²_____. We could see the ³_____ from our hotel. ⁴_____ are camels in the desert, but there ⁵_____ lakes.  We visited the ⁶_____ of Cairo – it's very busy! There ⁷_____ a volcano, but there is a very famous ⁸_____ – the Nile! Then we visited ⁹_____ friends in Alexandria.

**I CAN**

I can talk about countries using **is / isn't** and **some / aren't / any**.

I can ask and answer about places using **Is there a…?** and **Are there any…?**

I can write a friendly postcard.

# 5 Shopping

## 1 Look, find and circle.

| B | R | A | C | E | L | E | T | M | L |
|---|---|---|---|---|---|---|---|---|---|
| T | R | A | C | K | S | U | I | T | A |
| S | U | N | G | B | E | L | T | E | B |
| J | M | K | L | Q | M | L | A | L | E |
| P | B | T | O | D | B | L | V | L | L |
| O | R | F | V | A | Z | P | N | A | M |
| C | E | J | E | W | A | T | C | H | S |
| K | L | C | S | B | U | N | P | O | A |
| E | L | G | W | A | L | L | E | T | W |
| T | A | S | W | I | M | S | U | I | T |

## 2 Put the letters in order to make words.

1 bleal _____

2 stcirakut _____

3 koctep _____

4 tcahw _____

5 tleecarb _____

6 tebl _____

## 3 What are they going to buy? Listen and complete.

1 I'm going to buy that _____.

2 I'm going to buy those _____.

3 I'm going to buy that _____.

4 _____ that _____.

**4** **Read and circle.**

**1** Is ( you / he / they ) going to buy that watch? ✗

**2** Are ( we / he / I ) going to use this umbrella when it rains? ✓

**3** Are ( she / you / he ) going to wear this shirt to the party? ✗

**4** Is ( she / you / he ) going to put his wallet in his pocket? ✓

**5** Are ( they / I / he ) going to give the watch to someone as a present? ✓

**5** **Look at the questions, ticks (✓) and crosses (✗) in Activity 4. Make positive or negative statements.**

**1**  <u>He isn't going to buy that watch.</u>

**2**  _____

**3**  _____

**4**  _____

**5**  _____

**6** **Put the words in order to make sentences and questions.**

**1** going / to / am / I / buy / watch / a

<u>I am going to buy a watch.</u>

**2** you / are / swimsuit / going / take / to / your / ?

_____

**3** going / to / she / is / give / to / her / mum / it

_____

**4** contestant / going / win / to / is / the / ?

_____

**5** are / going / they / to / belt / buy / the / ?

_____

**7** Look and match.

a

b    £2

c

d    £199

e

f

| 1 | a cheap bracelet | b | 2 | an old-fashioned watch | |
| 3 | a modern watch | | 4 | an expensive bracelet | |
| 5 | baggy jeans | | 6 | a tight jumper | |

**8** Look and complete.

1

These trousers are too ____tight____.

2

That toy is _____.

3

This jumper _____.

4

These hats _____.

**9** Describe your things. Write sentences.

> baggy   floral   enough   colourful   modern
> too   old-fashioned   tight   expensive   big

My blue trousers are too tight. My umbrella is colourful.

_____

_____

**10**  **Listen and circle.**

Sky

Lee

**1** Sky is wearing ( her sister's / she / her ) jacket.

**2** Sky is wearing ( their / she / her ) baggy jeans.

**3** Lee is wearing ( him / his / he ) tight sweatshirt.

**4** Lee isn't wearing ( his / he / him ) belt. It is his ( dad's / mum's / brother's ) belt.

**11** **Complete. Whose is this?**

**1** This is Mary's bracelet. It is _____Mary's_____. It's _____hers_____.

**2** This is Harry's belt. It is _____. It's _____.

**3** These are Michael's and Louis's wallets. They are _____.
They're _____.

**4** That's my watch. It's _____.

**5** That umbrella belongs to us. It's _____.

**6** Those gloves belong to you. They're _____.

**12** **Think of items in your home. Write sentences about your and your family members' items.**

mine   his   hers   theirs

**1** The _____ belongs to me. It's _____.

**2** The _____ belongs to my _____. It's _____.

**3** These _____ belong to my _____. They're _____.

**4** The _____ belongs to my _____. It's _____.

**13** Read. Then number the pictures in order.

a Yes! Can you show us the way?

b Are you warm enough? No-o-o!

c I'm going to push her in the lake!

d We are going to go to the lake.

e HELP!!!

**14** Look at Activity 13 and write answers.

**1** Where are the explorers going to go? _____

**2** What is Smith going to do? _____

**3** Is Polly warm enough? _____

**15** What is the Queen going to buy? Listen and tick (✓) or cross (✗).

| 1 | hat | | 2 | scarf | | 3 | shoes | |
| 4 | belt | | 5 | dress | | | | |

**16** What should they wear? Read and tick (✓) or cross (✗).

**1**

I've got a family wedding this evening.

| | |
|---|---|
| a light blue dress | ✓ |
| blue flip-flops | ☐ |
| a white belt | ☐ |
| a baseball cap | ☐ |
| white shoes | ☐ |
| sunglasses | ☐ |
| a dark blue hat | ☐ |
| a gold bracelet | ☐ |
| a swimsuit | ☐ |

**2**

I've got my friend's party tonight.

| | |
|---|---|
| baggy trousers | ☐ |
| jeans | ☐ |
| a white shirt | ☐ |
| a dark green jacket | ☐ |
| a red belt | ☐ |
| black trainers | ☐ |
| shorts | ☐ |
| a black T-shirt | ☐ |
| sunglasses | ☐ |

**3**

I'm going walking in the mountains.

| | |
|---|---|
| tight jeans | ☐ |
| a baggy T-shirt | ☐ |
| sunglasses | ☐ |
| a warm jacket | ☐ |
| a yellow scarf | ☐ |
| sandals | ☐ |
| baggy shorts | ☐ |
| a baseball cap | ☐ |
| hiking boots | ☐ |

**17** Read and match.

Oh dear!   ~~Look!~~   Good afternoon!   Great choice!

**PHONICS & SPELLING**

| surprise | greeting | agreement | attracting attention |
|---|---|---|---|
|  | | | |
| _____ | _____ | _____ | Look! |

**18** Read and complete.

customers   department store   price   receipt   coupons

Being a clever consumer is important. ¹ <u>Customers</u> have many places to shop.
You can buy things in your local shop, at the market or in a ²_____. The same item
can have a different price in each place. You can do many things to save some money. Make sure
that you read advertisements and check the ³_____ online. Sometimes
you can also get a discount if you save ⁴_____. And always check your
⁵_____!

**19** Tick (✓) *Yes* or *No* for you.

## Are you a clever consumer?

**1** I'm good at saving money.
    Yes ☐    No ☐

**2** I write shopping lists.
    Yes ☐    No ☐

**3** I look for discounts.
    Yes ☐    No ☐

**4** I buy things when they are on sale.
    Yes ☐    No ☐

**5** I use coupons.
    Yes ☐    No ☐

**6** I research before buying.
    Yes ☐    No ☐

Mostly Yes: You are a clever consumer!
Some Yes and some No: You are on your way, but you can do more.
Mostly No: You need to plan to help save money.

**20** Look at Activity 19. What are you going to do? Write sentences.

1  <u>I am going to save more money.</u>
2  _____
3  _____
4  _____

# Wider World

**21** Write sentences using *going to*.

> bakery   floating market   pastries   vegetables
> garden   eat   buy   visit   grow

I am going to buy fresh bread at the bakery.

_____

_____

_____

**22** Read the information about Andreas. Then write a paragraph.

- parents are farmers
- grow and sell vegetables – carrots, potatoes, lettuce (only in winter), tomatoes, fruit (only in summer)
- Andreas sells vegetables at the Kalamata farmers' market every Saturday.
- set up stall, fruits and vegetables
- first customers come at around 7.00 a.m.
- sister give a few bags of vegetables to the food bank
- eat dinner at 7.00 p.m.
- relax and go to bed early

Andreas' parents are farmers. They sell their vegetables.

_____

_____

_____

_____

**23** **Read and match.**

**1**  a resolutions list

**2**  a shopping list

**3**  a to-do list

**4**  a present list

**5**  a reading list

**a**  a list of things you must do

**b**  a list of books to read

**c**  a list of things you want to do to make
        your life better

**d**  a list of presents you are going to give

**e**  a list of things you need to buy

**24** **Read and sort.**

> eggs   make cake   milk   100 Best Jokes   call Uncle Sid   fix car   bread
> Harry Potter and the Philosopher's Stone   The Cave Mystery

| 1 Shopping list | 2 To-do list | 3 Reading list |
| --- | --- | --- |
| _____ | _____ | _____ |
| _____ | _____ | _____ |
| _____ | _____ | |

**25** **Complete a list of things you are going to
do before your next birthday.**

- <u>I'm going to learn to skateboard.</u>
- _____
- _____
- _____
- _____
- _____

**WRITING TIP!**

We can use commas (,) to
separate three or more words,
e.g. *buy milk, biscuits, shampoo*

We can use a colon (:) to
introduce our list, e.g.
*Reading list:*

**26** **Number to make a dialogue.**

**a**  Are you going to take an umbrella for the sun? ☐

**b**  Yes, I am. What are you going to pack? ☐

**c**  I'm not going to take an umbrella, but I am going to take a hat. ☐

**d**  Are you going on the beach trip with school? ☐

**e**  I'm going to take my swimsuit – it's going to be hot! ☐

**27** **Listen and complete.**

My favourite bag is white with small letters on the ¹_____. It's really cool! My favourite shoes are my ²_____ ones. They're red and black. I don't like my winter boots because they're ³_____ and my summer shoes are ⁴_____ small now. I like my uniform. I really like the jacket. It's green and gold. ⁵_____ my favourite clothes.

**28** **Whose are these? Look and write sentences.**

1 Kay  2 Matt  3 Pablo  4 Tina

The dress is _____  _____  _____
Kay's. It's hers. _____  _____  _____

**I CAN**

I can use **going to** to indicate intention. ☐ ☐ ☐

I can talk about who clothing and accessories belong to. ☐ ☐ ☐

I can write a list for a specific purpose. ☐ ☐ ☐

# 6 Party time

**1** Write the verbs in the correct form.

| **YESTERDAY . . .** |
| --- |
| **1**   I _____*made*_____ (make) a sandwich for lunch. |
| **2**   I _____ (have) dinner at 6.00 p.m. |
| **3**   I _____ (come) to school by bus. |
| **4**   I _____ (give) my friend a present. |
| **5**   I _____ (see) my grandma. |
| **6**   I _____ (bring) my lunch to school. |
| **7**   I _____ (meet) my grandad. |
| **8**   I _____ (eat) curry. |
| **9**   I _____ (get) 100% in a test. |
| **10**   I _____ (sing) in a choir. |

**2** Complete the sentences.

**1**   Yesterday I _____*saw*_____ (see) my friend Kyle on his birthday.

**2**   He _____ (have) a party. It was fun!

**3**   I _____ (meet) Kyle's cousins at the party.

**4**   I _____ (bring) some games to play in the garden.

**5**   We _____ (eat) pizza and cake.

**6**   Kyle's mum _____ (make) the birthday cake.

**3** 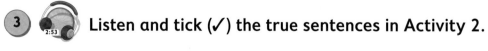 Listen and tick (✓) the true sentences in Activity 2.

1 ✓    2 ☐    3 ☐    4 ☐    5 ☐    6 ☐

## 4 Complete the paragraphs.

Robbie's party

Robbie [1] ___had___ (have) a birthday party in February. A lot of friends [2]_____ (come) to the party. They brought food, drinks and presents. Dan [3]_____ (give) Robbie a wallet for his birthday. Emma [4]_____ (not bring) didn't bring a present because she [5]_____ (make) a very big cake for Robbie.

Emma's party

Emma had a birthday party in July. Robbie brought a small cake and he [6]_____ (eat) all of it! It was sunny but Maddy [7]_____ (get) sunburnt because she brought an umbrella. Robbie [8]_____ (sing) songs to everyone and [9]_____ (make) them laugh. Everyone [10]_____ (have) a great time!

## 5 Make sentences.

1  Seven friends / come / Emma's party.  _____

2  Robbie / sing / songs.  _____

3  Emma / not give / Robbie a present.  _____

4  Everyone / have / a good time.  _____

## 6 Complete the sentences.

I [1] ___could blow out___ the candles when I [2]_____ two.

My brother [3]_____ when he [4]_____ one.

He [5]_____ his birthday cards when he [6]_____ five. When my parents [7]_____ two, they [8]_____ in English.

could read
couldn't speak
couldn't walk
could blow out
was (×3)
were

**7** **Read and find the mistakes. Then write correct sentences.**

**1** My cousin finished university and we had a farewell party.

<u>My cousin finished university and we had a graduation party.</u>

**2** There were lots of sandwiches, tea and cakes at the dinner party.

_____

**3** We said goodbye to our friends at their dinner party.

_____

**4** We dressed up as pirates for the graduation party.

_____

**5** We read scary stories and slept in sleeping bags at the dinner party.

_____

**8** **Complete the sentences.**

> dinner   wedding   picnic   surprise

**1** Last week I had a _____. We took our food to the park and ate outside.

**2** My cousin had a _____ party. She made pasta and salad.

**3** For my mum's 40th birthday we had a _____ party. She didn't know – Dad planned everything!

**4** When my cousin got married we went to their _____.

**9** **Think about a party you had. Write sentences.**

- What kind of party?
- What did you wear?
- What did you eat?
- What did you do?

I had a _____ party. _____

_____

_____

_____

**10** Read the table. Then answer the questions.

| Place | Date | Activities |
|-------|------|------------|
| China | July | go on a boat + see a film star |
| China | August | walk on the Great Wall of China |
| South Korea | September | meet some new friends + have a party |
| South Korea | October | go to an island + play on a beach |
| Japan | November | see a statue + eat a lot of fish |
| Japan | December | go on a fast train + climb Mount Fuji |

Last year my family went on a long holiday.

1   Where did they go in July?        They went to China.

2   What did they do in August?        _____

3   When did they go to Japan?        _____

4   Who did they meet in South Korea?        _____

**11** Look at Activity 10. Then write questions.

1   Where did they go in October?        (October) (where/go)?

2   _____ (Mount Fuji) (when/climb)?

3   _____ (November) (what/see)?

4   _____ (July) (who/see)?

**12** Put the words in order to make questions.

1   go / to / you / why / did / South Korea / ?        _____

2   she / go / when / did / Turkey / to / ?        _____

3   with / he / go / did / who / ?        _____

**13** **Read. Then number the pictures in order.**

**14** **Read and draw.**

There was a lake near a mountain. It was snowy. There were some trees on the mountain. There was ice over the lake. There were two explorers fishing in a hole in the ice. Mike and Polly were there, too. They were all singing. Gizmo played with a red ribbon.

**15** **Read and circle.**

**1**  I don't know the meaning of a word. I should
( go to school / use a dictionary ).

**2**  I'm not good at writing. ( I should / shouldn't ) write about things I like.

**3**  I haven't got any money to buy a birthday present. I should ( buy / make ) a birthday card.

**4**  I want to play football. I'm not good at it. I should ( run / play ) for fun.

**5**  I've got a test and I feel nervous. I should ( study / watch television ) with a friend.

**6**  I can't remember vocabulary easily. I should ( write / answer ) lists of new words.

**16** **Read and match.**

| | | | |
|---|---|---|---|
| **1** | Where did you go? | **a** | I arrived at four o'clock. |
| **2** | Who did she see? | **b** | No, they couldn't. |
| **3** | Could they go to the party? | **c** | Yes, they are. |
| **4** | Are they staying late? | **d** | I went to my uncle's wedding. |
| **5** | When did you arrive? | **e** | Yes, she did. |
| **6** | Did she bring any presents? | **f** | She saw her friends. |

**17** **Look at Activity 16 and complete the table.**

| Yes/No QUESTIONS (rising intonation) ↗ | Wh- QUESTIONS (falling intonation) ↘ |
|---|---|
| | Where did you go? |
| | |
| | |

**18** Read and complete.

landed   Native Americans   crossed   months   celebrated   voyage

### Diary of a Settler

Our journey from England to North America was very difficult. We ¹ _____crossed_____ the ocean on a ship called the Mayflower. The first part of the ² _____ was fine, but then there were very strong storms. We ³ _____ in the new world after 62 days. That is more than two ⁴ _____ at sea. We couldn't find food, but we met some ⁵ _____ who helped us.

Today we are going to ⁶ _____ with our Native American friends!

**19** Write the verbs in the correct form.

**1** The settlers __crossed__ (cross) the dangerous ocean.

**2** The settlers _____ (land) in winter.

**3** It _____ (is) very cold and foggy when they arrived.

**4** The settlers _____ (learn) about farming.

**5** The settlers _____ (give) thanks to the Native Americans.

**20** Think of a celebration in your country. Complete the table and the sentences.

| | |
|---|---|
| **Name of country:** _____ | **Special food/drink:** _____ |
| **Name of celebration:** _____ | **Why celebrated:** _____ |
| **When celebrated:** _____ | **Why I like it:** _____ |

In _____ (country) we celebrate _____ (name of the celebration). We always have a party on _____ (month/day). It is a great day.

We have _____ (special food and drinks). We celebrate _____ (name of the celebration) because _____.

I like _____ (name of celebration) because _____.

# Wider World

**21** Read and complete.

chef   edible   ~~variety~~   vegetarian

**1**   I like this restaurant because it's got a good __variety__ of food.

**2**   I only eat fruit, dairy and vegetables because I'm a _____.

**3**   I didn't know that some flowers are _____.

**4**   I want to be a famous _____ and work in the best restaurants.

**22** Read and match.

**1**   Hi, Denise. What did you do last night?

**2**   Where is this restaurant?

**3**   What does it look like?

**4**   What did you eat?

**5**   Did you like it?

**a**   There isn't a lot of variety on the menu. I had pasta and salad.

**b**   We went to the new restaurant.

**c**   It's by the sea.

**d**   Yes, the food was delicious and I enjoyed watching the chef prepare the food in front of me.

**e**   It's a cave. It's really different.

**23** Imagine you visited a unusual restaurant by the sea.  Use the questions in Activity 22 to write about it.

I went to a restaurant _____ (when). It was in _____ (place).

_____

_____

_____

_____

**24** Tick (✓) the things we write in an invitation.

**1** our address ✓  **2** our phone number / email ☐

**3** what presents to bring ☐  **4** the time of the party ☐

**5** date of the party ☐  **6** the type of party ☐

**7** our favourite food ☐  **8** what music you will play ☐

**25** Read and think. Which invitation has got the complete information?

**1**

Hi Oliver,

I'm having a party. Come at 6.00 p.m.

My number is 567-324-764.

See you there.

Maria

**2**

Hey, Noah.

My fancy dress party is on Saturday, 5th May.

It's at 56 Miles Street, Westfield.

It starts at 7.30 p.m.

Call me – 324 674

Hope you can come.

Luna.

**26** What is missing from the incorrect invitation? Write.

_____

_____

**27** Imagine you are having a party. Complete the invitation.

**WRITING TIP!**

Make sure your invitation includes all the important information.
- What party • When it is • Where it is
- What time it starts/finishes
- What to bring • Who to contact

**POOL party**

Dear _____,

Please come to my party on _____.

It's a _____ party.

It's at _____.

It starts at _____.

Call me for directions – _____.

Hope to see you there.

_____

**28 Read and match.**

| dinner party   farewell party   picnic   surprise party   wedding |

**1** a party you don't know about

_____

**2** two people get married

_____

**3** people sit down and eat and drink at this party _____

**4** a goodbye party for someone who is leaving _____

**5** a party outside with food, often in a park _____

**29 Read and circle.**

Yesterday, I ¹( went / brought ) to a birthday party. I ²( made / met ) some old friends and ³( make / made ) lots of new friends. We ⁴( had / didn't have ) the party inside, it was a picnic in the park. We ⁵( didn't sing / not sing ) karaoke but we ⁶( played / play ) lots of games. We each ⁷( bring / brought ) some food but we ⁸( didn't ate / didn't eat ) it all!

**30 Put the words in order to make questions. Then look at Activity 29 and answer.**

**1** was / birthday / party / When / the / ?

_____

**2** was / the / birthday / Where / party / ?

_____

**3** What / they / do / the / did / party / at ?

_____

**I CAN**

I can talk about what did or didn't happen in the past.

I can ask and answer about past events.

I can write an invitation to a party.

# 7 School

**1**  **Listen and complete.**

scary  boring  ~~easy~~  difficult  funny  romantic
interesting  exciting  embarrassing  important

The first lesson at school was ¹_____easy_____. I forgot my homework and it was
²_____. The second and third lessons were ³_____. There was an
⁴_____ game in the fourth lesson. Lunch was ⁵_____. The lessons
after lunch were ⁶_____. In the last lesson, we read some poems. Some were
⁷_____, some were ⁸_____ and some were ⁹_____.
There was an ¹⁰_____ note from the teachers for our parents.

**2** **Listen and write for Sarah. Use words from Activity 1.**

**1** Dinosaurs

Sarah: ___interesting___

You: _____

**2** PENS AND PENCILS

Sarah: _____

You: _____

**3** Anna and the Aliens

Sarah: _____

You: _____

**4** First Book of Words
🐱 cat
🏠 house
🐶 dog

Sarah: _____

You: _____

**5** Fun with Numbers

Sarah: _____

You: _____

**6** The Adventures of 009

Sarah: _____

You: _____

**3** **Now complete Activity 2 for you.**

**4** **Read and match.**

My first day at school was scary. I was only five and there were a lot of big children in the school. I couldn't find my class and it was embarrassing. The lessons were very difficult. My teacher was kind but I was very sad! There was an important lesson about safety in the class.

**1**  Was Emma's first day at school scary?      **a**  No, she wasn't.

**2**  Was she four?     **b**  Yes, he was.

**3**  Were there a lot of big children?     **c**  Yes, it was.

**4**  Were the lessons easy?     **d**  No, they weren't.

**5**  Was her teacher kind?     **e**  Yes, there was.

**6**  Was there an important lesson?     **f**  Yes, there were.

**5** **What was your first day at school like? Put the words in order to make questions. Then write answers.**

**1**  you / five / were / years old  <u>Were you five years old</u> ?

_____ .

**2**  your / kind / was / teacher _____ ?

_____ .

**3**  scary / it / was _____ ?

_____ .

**4**  you / were / happy _____ ?

_____ .

**6** **Write about the first time you did your favourite sport.**

- Was it exciting/scary/easy/difficult/embarrassing?
- Were you happy?

<u>The first time I played tennis was very exciting. I was very happy.</u>

_____

_____

**7** 🎧 3:14 **Look and write sentences. Then listen and circle _T_ (True) or _F_ (False).**

**1** ⚽ + 🌐 ✔ boring    <u>Sport and Geography were boring.</u>    T / (F)

**2** 🌐 ✘ easy    _____    T / F

**3** 🎻 + 🎹 ✔ fun    _____    T / F

**4** 🧮 ✘ interesting    _____    T / F

**5** 🧪 + 💻 ✘ difficult    _____    T / F

**6** 🎨 ✔ exciting    _____    T / F

**8** **Write sentences for you.**

> Last year, Maths wasn't easy.

| interesting   boring   exciting   funny   difficult   easy |

| last year<br>this year | Maths   Drama   Design   Sport<br>Computer Studies   Music |

**1** _____

**2** _____

**3** _____

**4** _____

**9** **Think about your lessons last week. Write sentences.**

**1** Science was _____ .

**2** Maths _____ .

**3** _____

**10**  **Listen and circle. Then answer the questions.**

| Jacob's homework and sports diary | | | | |
|---|---|---|---|---|
| **Monday** | **Tuesday** | **Wednesday** | **Thursday** | **Friday** |
| Maths <br> Computer Studies | History <br> Swimming | English <br> Science | Trampolining <br> Art | Music <br> Sport |

**1** Did Jacob have Computer Studies homework on Monday?  <u>Yes, he did.</u>

**2** Did Jacob go swimming on Tuesday?  _____

**3** Did Jacob have English homework on Wednesday?  _____

**4** Did Jacob go trampolining on Thursday?  _____

**5** Did Jacob have Music homework on Friday?  _____

**11** **Read and write questions. Then circle.**

| Zoey's homework and sports diary | | | | |
|---|---|---|---|---|
| **Monday** | **Tuesday** | **Wednesday** | **Thursday** | **Friday** |
| Music | English | swimming | Maths | Art |
| exciting ✓ | boring ✗ | difficult ✓ | easy ✗ | interesting ✗ |

**1** <u>Did Zoey have Music on Monday?</u> _____

Yes, Zoey had Music on Monday. It ( (was) / wasn't ) exciting.

**2** _____?

No, Zoey didn't have Maths on Tuesday. She had ( Art / English ). It wasn't boring.

**3** _____?

Yes, Zoey went swimming on Wednesday. It was ( difficult / easy ).

**4** _____?

Yes, Zoey had Maths on Thursday. It wasn't ( difficult / easy ).

**5** _____?

No, Zoey didn't go to the park on Friday. She had Art. It ( was / wasn't ) interesting.

**13** Read. Then number the pictures in order.

a Quick, when's Science?

b This is a tunnel to Bollington Hall.

c What's the code?

d Phew! We did it!

e We're at Bollington Hall.

All the lights are on!

f It's a school timetable!

**14** Look at Activity 13. Then read and circle.

**1**  ( Polly / A police officer / The Police Chief ) goes into the tunnel first.

**2**  Polly finds ( the diamonds / a key / a school timetable ) in the tunnel.

**3**  They can't go on without a ( poem / code / rope ).

**4**  It is ( morning / afternoon / night ) when they come out of the tunnel.

**15** Look at Activity 13 and tick (✓).

**1**  Who is having a party?

a     b     c

**2**  Who got the code right?

a     b     c

**16** Listen and write answers.

**1** Did Grandma like diving?

Yes, she did.

**2** Was there a swimming pool at Grandma's school?

**3** Was Grandma a scientist?

**4** Did Grandma go to Poland?

**5** Where did Grandma go?

 **17** Listen and circle the word with the different ending.

**PHONICS & SPELLING**

| | | |
|---|---|---|
| **1** played | followed | ~~fixed~~ |
| **2** landed | cooked | painted |
| **3** followed | fixed | cooked |
| **4** followed | played | landed |

**18** Write in the correct column.

liked   landed   cleaned   spelled   watched   wanted
ended   snowed   stayed   painted   laughed   hoped

| /t/ | /d/ | /ɪd/ |
|---|---|---|
|  |  |  |
|  |  |  |
|  |  |  |
|  |  |  |

**19** **Read and match.**

| | | | | |
|---|---|---|---|---|
| **1** | spread | **a** | a sound you make from your throat when you are ill |
| **2** | cough | **b** | this makes you feel tired and gives you a temperature |
| **3** | germs | **c** | you can't see them but they make you ill |
| **4** | virus | **d** | you do this to your hands with water and soap |
| **5** | flu | **e** | when a germ goes from one place to another |
| **6** | scrub | **f** | headaches, temperature, tiredness are all ... |
| **7** | symptoms | **g** | flu is a type of this |

**20** **Look and write.**

scrub our hands   sneeze into a tissue   cough into our elbows
eat healthy food   exercise

1 _____

2 _____

3 _____

4 _____

5 _____

**21** **Read and circle *T* (True) or *F* (False).**

| | | |
|---|---|---|
| **1** | It's important that we always wash our hands. | (T)/ F |
| **2** | We should wash the front and back of our hands. | T / F |
| **3** | We must touch our faces, noses and mouths. | T / F |
| **4** | We should sneeze and cough in the air. | T / F |
| **5** | We should go out as much as possible when we are ill. | T / F |
| **6** | We should eat lots of healthy food and exercise. | T / F |

# Wider World

**22** **Complete the sentences.**

> activities   boarding   cultures   international   study

1   We _____ hard every day so we can be good students.

2   I have a lot of after school _____ – sports, music and languages.

3   I don't think I could go to a _____ school - I would miss my family.

4   I enjoy learning about different _____ from around the world.

5   She goes to an _____ school with children from all over the world.

**23** **Read and write answers.**

**Bangladesh Boat Schools**

Bangladesh has got unusual schools. It has got boat schools. Each boat is a classroom for 30 students. Flood water can make it difficult for children to get to school, so the boats are very important. The boats get their electricity from the sun. They have laptops, internet connections and small libraries. The boats pick up the children before school, then they take them home when lessons have finished. It is important that students get an education.

1   What is unusual about these schools in Bangladesh?

   _____.

2   Where do they get their electricity from?

   _____.

3   How many students can each boat teach?

   _____.

4   Why are these schools important?

   _____.

**24** Read and complete.

**Tilly Merlin**

16th June

Mum, please can you order a book for my birthday? It's called *The Queen's Hat* and it's £5.50. Don't forget, my birthday is in two weeks! Thanks

| City Book Shop Online Order | |
|---|---|
| Date of order: | ¹ 16th June |
| ² _____ | Joanne Merlin |
| ³ _____ | 2 Riley Street, Norwich |
| Name of book: | ⁴ _____ |
| Price: | ⁵ _____ |

**25** Read and write the answers.

To: Julie, School office
From: Lucas French

Hi Julie,

Can you order some new sci-fi books for my class?

I've already got *Space Run 202* by T S Estille so only order *Moon Travel* by Cathy Rooms and *Sun Planets* by Danny King. They cost £6.00 each.

Thanks,

Lucas French.

To: Lucas French
From: Julie, School Office

Hello Lucas,

I'm going to order *The History of Rocks* by Joanne Carter for Class 4G today. It also costs £6.00. I can order your books, too.

Best wishes,

Julie Brett
Mascot School,
George Road,
Exeter

**1** What does Lucas want to order? _____

**2** What does Julie order? _____

**26** Look at Activity 25 and complete the order form.

**WRITING TIP!**

Customer = first name and surname
Address = house number, street name and town
Name of book = title
Author = who wrote the book

| City Book Shop Order Form | |
|---|---|
| Date: | ¹ _____ |
| Customer: | ² Julie |
| Address: | ³ _____ |
| Name of book(s) and author(s): | ⁴ _____ |
| Total: | ⁵ _____ |

**27** **Read and match.**

boring   exciting   funny   scary

**1**  jokes should be like this _____

**2**  not interesting _____

**3**  a good, fun feeling _____

**4**  dark places can be this _____

**28** **Put the words in order to make questions. Then write answers for you.**

**1**  you / Did / Maths / have / yesterday / ?

_____

**2**  interesting  / Were / on / last / TV / there / any / programmes / night / ?

_____

**29** **Read and write the school subject.**

**1**  studying acting _____

**2**  studying countries_____

**3**  studying the past _____

**4**  studying instruments _____

**30** **Read and complete. Then listen and check.**

**David:**  My school was special. It ¹_____ a tennis school.

**Interviewer:**  ²_____ there other lessons, too?

**David:**  Yes, there were – Maths, Science, English and History. But they ³_____ only in the morning. There ⁴_____ tennis lessons every afternoon.

**Interviewer:**  ⁵_____ it a good school?

**David:**  Yes, it was. We ⁶_____ very happy there!

**I CAN**

I can ask and answer past simple questions.

I can ask and answer questions about past activities.

I can complete a form with information from a text.

**1** Complete the crossword with the nationalities.

**ACROSS**

**1** Argentina

**3** Egypt

**6** Brazil

**7** The United States

**8** Italy

**9** Spain

**12** China

**13** ~~the United Kingdom~~

**DOWN**

**1** Australia

**2** Mexico

**4** Turkey

**5** Japan

**10** Poland

**11** South Korea

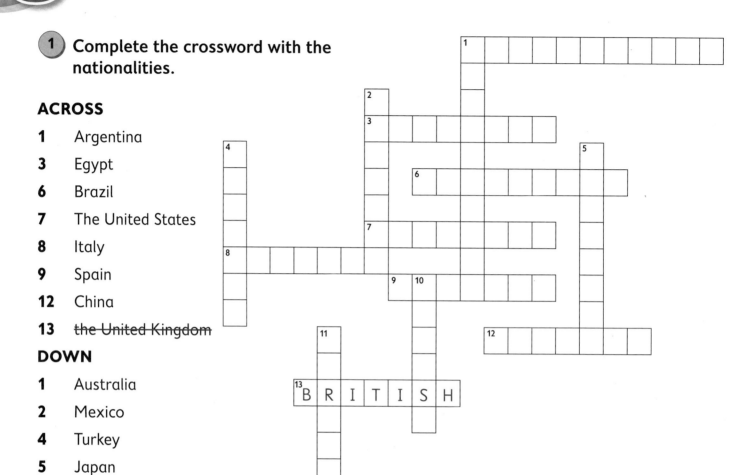

13 B R I T I S H

**2** Look, listen and complete the table.

| Job | Famous person | Nationality |
|---|---|---|
| footballer | Lionel Messi | |
| writer | | |
| singer | | |
| tennis player | | |
| actor | | |

International Cooking Contest

a Italy

b China

c Brazil

d Argentina

e Egypt

f the United Kingdom

**4** **Look at Activity 3 and complete the sentences.**

**1** Where's she from? She's from _the United Kingdom_ . She's _____.

**2** Is he Brazilian? _____. He's from Brazil. He's _____.

**3** Is she Egyptian? _____. She's from _____.
She's _____.

**4** Where's he from? He's from _____. He's _____.

**5** Is she from Argentina? _____. She's from _____.
She's _____.

**6** Where's he from? He's from _____. He's _____.

**5** Put the letters in order to make words.

1   taiewr   _____

2   scitisten   _____

3   cinmeahc   _____

4   anmssbuenis   _____

5   irnegeen   _____

6   VT resentper   _____

7   cinauism   _____

8   ralios   _____

9   racto   _____

10   oobftarell   _____

11   bisessunoawmn   _____

**6** Look and write sentences.

1

The United Kingdom

She's a musician.
She's from the United Kingdom.
She's a British musician.

2

Italy

_____
_____
_____

3

Mexico

_____
_____
_____

4

Japan

_____
_____
_____

**7** 🎧 3:38 **Listen and number.**

**8** **Read and match with the photos. Then complete the sentences.**

**A** He's ¹ ___Chinese___ .

He's the man ² _____ plays basketball in the United States.

A film ³ _____ was made in 2004 tells the story of his first year in the National Basketball Association.

**B** Was she ⁴ _____?

Yes, she was. Egypt is the country ⁵_____ she was Queen.

In 51 BC she was the woman ⁶_____ ruled Egypt.

A film ⁷_____ was made in 1999 tells Cleopatra's life story.

She is the queen ⁸ _____ is famous for bathing in milk.

**C** Where's he from?

He's from Brazil. He's ⁹ _____ .

He's the footballer ¹⁰ _____ Brazilians call King Pele.

*Pelé: Birth of a Legend* is the film ¹¹ _____ they made in 2016 about his life.

**9** Read. Then number the pictures in order.

a — "I'm going to get those kids!" / "Help!"

b — "Extraordinary!"

c — "Thank you! All kids should be like you."

d — "Quick! Catch them!"

e — "The diamonds are in the ice!"

f — "Where are they from?" / "Is this a fancy dress party?"

**10** Look at Activity 9 and match.

| | | | | |
|---|---|---|---|---|
| **1** | How does the Queen feel? | | **a** | The Police Chief. |
| **2** | What does Mike do? | | **b** | The Queen. |
| **3** | How do Frost and Smith feel? | | **c** | She is excited. |
| **4** | Who says, 'Extraordinary!'? | | **d** | He finds the diamonds. |
| **5** | Where are the diamonds? | | **e** | They feel angry and scared. |
| **6** | Who says, 'Quick! Catch them!'? | | **f** | They're in the ice wall. |

**11** Look and complete the sentences.

I'm [1] _____British_____ .
I'm from [2] _____ .
Where [3] _____ ?

I'm a Martian. [4] _____ from the planet [5] _____ .

Yes, I am. I'm from [9] _____ .

[6] _____ Polish?

No, I'm not. I'm from Ice Island. [7] _____ are you from?
[8] _____ Italian?

**12** **Read and complete the chart. Who is the best role model?**

**Gwyneth** always works hard at school and often arrives on time. Her mother works all day so Gwyneth usually helps a lot around the house. She cleans her room and makes breakfast for her younger brother.

**VALUES**

Be a good role model for others.

**Harry** is usually on time but is sometimes late for class. He sometimes works hard at school and sometimes helps at home, but he really likes watching films.

**Rob** is always on time. He usually works hard at school and does his homework. He often helps at home. He takes out the rubbish and cleans his room.

|  | |
| a = always | u = usually |
| s = sometimes | o = often |
|  | n = never |

|  | arrives on time | works hard at school | helps at home |
|---|---|---|---|
| Gwyneth | o |  |  |
| Rob |  |  |  |
| Harry |  |  |  |

The best role model is _____.

**13** 🎧 3:42 **Listen and circle the short vowels.**

| | | | | |
|---|---|---|---|---|
| **1** | pen | (leg) | web | free |
| **2** | time | five | sit | mine |
| **3** | take | hat | make | date |
| **4** | rose | note | sock | toe |

**PHONICS & SPELLING**

**14** **Write the words from Activity 13 in the correct column for a–o. Think of a word in each column for u. Then say.**

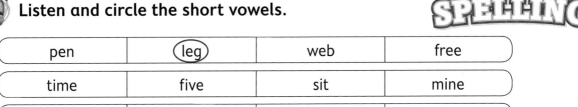

| LONG vowel | SHORT vowel |
|---|---|
| a    take | a |
| e | e |
| i | i |
| o | o |
| u | u |

**15** Read and match.

| | | | | |
|---|---|---|---|---|
| **1** | invent | **a** | a person who creates things |
| **2** | construct | **b** | to think and plan how something will work |
| **3** | design | **c** | a thought or suggestion |
| **4** | idea | **d** | to make or build something |
| **5** | inventor | **e** | to make something completely new |

**16** Read and circle.

**1**   It was a Frenchman ( what / when / who ) invented the first alarm clock.

**2**   Basketball is a sport ( that / what / where ) many people like.

**3**   The ballpoint pen was invented by two journalists ( which / when / who )  had problems writing.

**4**   A digital watch is a great invention ( when / that / this ) tells the time.

**5**   A mobile phone is a device ( what / which / who ) makes phonecalls.

**6**   Basketball was invented in a place ( where / when / what ) it is very cold in the winter.

**7**   An inventor is a person ( who / what / which ) creates completely new things.

**17**   Think of your own invention. Write a description.

Name of the invention: _____.

In _____ (date) I invented the _____ (name of invention).

A _____ (name) is something that you can use to _____.

People who like _____ need a _____ (name).

You can use a _____ (name) when you _____.

Normally, the best place to use it is where you _____.

A _____ (name) is an amazing thing which everyone should have!

# Wider World

**18** **Match the words with the definitions.**

1   email

2   website

3   instant messaging

4   video call

**a**   sending electronic messages in real time using the internet

**b**   when you can see and speak to someone in a different place by using the internet

**c**   a place on the internet for finding information

**d**   message or letter we send through the internet

**19** **Read and find the mistakes. Then write correct sentences.**

1   Some Australean children have lessons over the internet.

<u>Some Australian children have lessons over the internet.</u>

2   Students talk to a teacher which is in a different place.

_____

3   Doctors video calls to treat patients use.

_____

4   Instant messaging apps are often used by people what want to send videos and pictures.

_____

5   There is a website when distance-learning students can chat.

_____

**20** **What do you use the internet for? Write four sentences.**

1   _____

2   _____

3   _____

4   _____

**21** Which is a list of instructions? Read and tick (✓).

**1**

To do:
- Feed cat
- Take dog for walk
- Make sandwiches
- Finish Science project
- Help Dad in garden ☐

**2**

How to print a file:
- Turn on the printer.
- Open the document.
- Click on <u>File</u>.
- Choose <u>Print</u>.
- Take your pages from the printer. ☐

**22** Read and order from 1 to 7.

## How to download music

**a** Click on 'albums' or 'songs' ☐

**b** Go to a music web player ☐

**c** Pay for the song or album ☐

**d** Click on the menu 'music library' ☐

**e** Choose the song or album you want to download ☐

**f** Save to your phone or computer ☐

**WRITING TIP!**

We can use the sequencing words *First*, *Then*, *Next* and *Finally* to help order our instructions.

**23** What must we do when we write a list of instructions? Tick (✓).

**1** Give very long instructions. ☐

**2** Tell jokes. ☐

**3** Give instructions in the correct order. ☐

**4** Explain everything. ☐

**5** Be concise. ☐

**6** Don't number instructions. ☐

**24** Think of something that needs a list of instructions to explain how to use it. Write.

_____

_____

**25** **Match the words with the definitions.**

> a British footballer   a Japanese waiter   an American mechanic
> an Egyptian engineer   an Italian actor

**1**   a person from the United States who
fixes cars _____

**2**   a person who serves people in
restaurants and who is from country in
Asia _____

**3**   a person who is from a country in North
Africa _____

**4**   an athlete who is from country in Europe
_____

**5**   a person from Europe who acts in the
theatre _____

**26** **Look at Activity 25 and answer the questions.**

**1**   Who's from the United States? _____

**2**   Is the footballer from Italy? _____

**3**   Are the engineer and the waiter from Europe? _____

**27** **Read and circle.**

**1**   Marie is the woman ( who / which ) works in the library.

**2**   I am from a country ( which / where ) there are many forests.

**3**   This is the car ( that / who ) my dad drives.

**28** **Which invention do you think is very useful? Write sentences.**

The invention I find useful is _____.

It can _____.

I think it is useful because _____

_____.

> • What is the invention called?
> • What does it do?
> • Why is it useful?

**I CAN**

I can ask and answer about nationalities.

I can talk about people, places and things using, **who**, **where**, **that** and **which**.

I can write instructions.

## Goodbye

**1** **Look. Then read and write.**

**1** What's his name? _____

**2** What's _____?
He's good at playing football and finding thieves.

**3** What's her name? _____

**4** What's _____?
She's good at finding thieves.

**2** **Read and match.**

**1** They are good at eating ice cream ☐

**2** She thinks Mike and Polly are clever. ☐

**3** She thinks police work is important. ☐

**4** They think prison is boring. They aren't friendly. ☐

**5** They think fishing is interesting. ☐

**3** 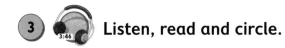 **Listen, read and circle.**

**1**  Tyler thinks the book was ( interesting / exciting ).

**2**  First, he sounded ( funny / scary ) when he practised his pronunciation.

**3**  Lucy thinks the book was ( helpful / exciting ).

**4**  She is going to dress up as ( Gizmo / Polly ).

---

**Ice Island: Book Report**

**Tyler:** I really liked this Ice Island course book. It was very interesting, and I learnt lots of new English.

My favourite part of each unit was the phonics. I liked listening to the sounds and I liked practising. At first, I usually sounded very funny, but then I got better. Pronunciation is important, and I'm good at it now! What do you think, Lucy?

**Lucy:** Thanks, Tyler, that was helpful. I've learnt lots of English!  The course book was exciting. I liked the Ice Island story.  My favourite character was Gizmo. He was very clever! I am going to go to a fancy dress party soon. I am going to dress up as Polly!

---

**4** **Complete with the correct form of the verbs.**

The Ice Island story [1]_____ (is) very exciting!  I [2]_____ (like)
Polly and Mike. They [3]_____ (are) hard-working. My favourite character
[4]_____ (is) Gizmo!  He [5]_____ (is) very clever!  I liked it when
Mike [6]_____ (see) the diamonds. The Queen was very happy when she
[7]_____ (get) her diamonds back!

---

**5** **Think about your favourite book. Complete the book report.**

My favourite book is called _____ (title). It is by _____ (author).

I like it because it is _____. My favourite character(s) is/are _____

_____ because he/she/they is/are _____.

I liked it when _____.

## 6 🎧 3:48 Listen and write.

| | | | |
|---|---|---|---|
| 1 | March | 1 | _____ |
| 2 | 2 _____ | | Spain |
| 3 | April | 3 | _____ |
| 4 | 4 _____ | | Mexico |
| 5 | 5 _____ | | Argentina |
| 6 | June | 6 | _____ |

## 7 Complete the school timetable for you. What do you think about each school subject? Write sentences.

| | Monday | Tuesday | Wednesday | Thursday | Friday |
|---|---|---|---|---|---|
| morning | | | | | |
| afternoon | | | | | |

easy   difficult   interesting   boring

**1** I think that _____ is _____.

**2** _____.

**3** _____.

**4** _____.

## 8 What is your daily routine like? Complete the sentences.

**1** I always _____.

**2** I usually _____.

**3** I often _____.

**4** I sometimes _____.

**5** I never _____.

**9** **Complete the sentences for you.**

**1** Yesterday, I _____ .

**2** Yesterday, I didn't _____ .

**10** **Draw or stick a picture of your favourite place. Then describe it.**

There's a _____ .

There isn't a _____ .

There are some _____ .

There aren't any _____ .

**11** **Draw or stick a picture of your favourite famous person. Then write.**

What does he/she look like?

_____

Why do you like him/her?

_____

What is he/she good at?

_____

Where is he/she from?

_____

This is _____ .

( He's / She's ) ( a / an ) _____ .

# Halloween

**1** 🎧 3:50 **Look, listen and colour. Then write.**

**2** **Read and match. Then write.**

> caramel corn   apple bobbing   scary story   pumpkin bread

**1** This is a game you play at Halloween with apples in water. _____

**2** This is something you read. _____

**3** This is a bread you eat, made with an orange vegetable. _____

**4** This is sweet food that you eat. _____

**3** **Complete the party invitation.**

HALLOWEEN INVITATION

Dear _____,

_____

Place: _____

Time: _____

# Christmas

**1** **Read and complete.**

Christmas Day is <sup>1</sup>_____ the 25th of December and there are two weeks <sup>2</sup>_____ school holidays. My favourite thing <sup>3</sup>_____ Christmas is the music. I'm in a music club <sup>4</sup>_____ school and <sup>5</sup>_____ the evenings before Christmas we sing Christmas carols outside the shops. It's cold and dark <sup>6</sup>_____ we love it.

<sup>7</sup>_____ the 24th of December, I hang a stocking <sup>8</sup>_____ the living room. The <sup>9</sup>_____ the morning, it's got presents in it. Some children think the presents are <sup>10</sup>_____ Father Christmas.

We eat a big lunch <sup>11</sup>_____ Christmas Day with Granny and Grandad: turkey, potatoes <sup>12</sup>_____ Brussel sprouts. Then we eat a fruit pudding called Christmas pudding. After the meal, there are presents <sup>13</sup>_____ everyone.

**2** **Answer the questions.**

**1** When is Christmas Day?

_____

**2** What do people sing at Christmas?

_____

**3** Where do children hang stockings?

_____

**4** What do people in the United Kingdom eat on Christmas Day?

_____

**5** What do you call Father Christmas in your country?

_____

## 1 Listen and answer the questions.

**1** How much milk does Josh use? _____ ml

**2** How many eggs does Josh use? _____

**3** How much flour does Josh use? _____ g

**4** How much melted butter does Josh beat? _____ g

## 2 Complete the recipe.

### Josh's banana chocolate pancake

Pour the ¹_____ into a jug and add
²_____ eggs – ³_____ well.

Put ⁴_____ into a bowl. ⁵_____ the egg and milk mixture into the centre of the flour. Beat the melted ⁶_____ into the batter.

Heat the frying pan and pour some ⁷_____ for each pancake and leave to cook for
⁸_____ minutes. Toss the ⁹_____.

When your pancake is cooked, add bananas and chocolate syrup. Happy Pancake day!

## 3 Invent something to eat. Write the recipe.

**Ingredients**

_____

_____

_____

**Recipe**

_____

_____

_____

# April Fools' Day

**1** 🎧 **Listen. Then answer the questions.**

**1**  Who played the practical joke? _____

**2**  Did the class think they were participating in the contest? _____

**3**  Were the children disappointed when they understood the joke? _____

**4**  Did they think it was a joke from the beginning? _____

**2** **Read and match.**

**1**  When do people celebrate April Fools' Day in the United Kingdom?

**2**  Where do they celebrate it?

**3**  What do people do to celebrate this festival?

**4**  When do people in Mexico and Spain celebrate something similar?

**a**  They play pranks and jokes on people.

**b**  28th December

**c**  1st April

**d**  It is celebrated in Australia, Brazil, Italy, Poland, the United Kingdom and the United States.

**3** **Think about the last prank or joke you played on a friend. Answer the questions.**

**1**  When did you play it? _____

**2**  Where did you play it? _____

**3**  Why did you play it? _____

**4**  Who did you play it on? _____

**5**  What did you do? _____

# Extra Practice

## Welcome

**1** What time is it? Look and write.

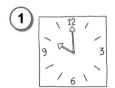      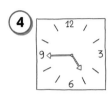

1 _____

2 _____

3 _____

4 _____

**2** Find and circle the days of the week.

HIMONDAYITISTUESDAYANDWEDNESDAYNOTHURSDAYYESFRIDAYSITSATURDAYANDSUNDAY

**3** Read and complete.

> dancing   listened   played   reading   watched

1 I _____ with John yesterday.

2 I am _____ a book now.

3 At lunchtime I _____ to music.

4 They _____ TV yesterday.

5 Mary is _____ with Tony now.

**4** Answer the questions for you.

What did you do yesterday? _____

_____

What are you doing now? _____

_____

# Unit 1

**1** Put the letters in order to make words.

**1** ndki _____

**2** radk _____

**3** dnolbe _____

**4** yssob _____

**5** elcrev _____

**6** hys _____

**7** tecu _____

**8** eautibulf _____

**2** Think about a family member. Answer the questions.

What does he/she look like? _____

_____

What is he/she like? _____

_____

**3** Read and find the mistakes. Then write correct sentences.

**1** My sister is blonde hair and has got very bossy.

<u>My sister has got blonde hair and is very bossy.</u>

**2** John hasn't got sporty. He isn't curly hair.

_____

**3** My grandad is moustache but he's bald. He's got clever and talkative.

_____

**4** Julio's dog is dark hair and has got friendly.

_____

**5** Mark has got kind and isn't curly hair.

_____

# Unit 2

**1** Read and match.

| | | | | |
|---|---|---|---|---|
| **1** | make | **a** | my homework |
| **2** | tidy | **b** | my bed |
| **3** | revise | **c** | in class |
| **4** | take notes | **d** | my room |
| **5** | be | **e** | on time |
| **6** | do | **f** | for a test |

**2** Is it good advice? Read and tick (✓) or cross (✗).

**1** You must never do sports.                    **✗**

**2** You should always recycle.                    _____

**3** You should usually help at home.              _____

**4** You should never brush your teeth.            _____

**5** You should always be good.                    _____

**3** What advice can you give? Read and write sentences.

**1** I've got a test tomorrow.

_____

**2** My bedroom is always untidy.

_____

**3** I'm always tired in the morning.

_____

# Unit 3

**1** **Find the words.**

DRESSPLAYINGCHESSTRETHROWINGRUWRITINGSTORIESANDIVINGINTSINGINGKARAOKEVIDGAMEDRAWINGDINGROLLERBLADINGI

**2** **Read and circle.**

**1** ( Dive / Diving ) is fun.

**2** ( Writing / Write ) stories relaxes me.

**3** Do you have ( singing / sing ) lessons at school?

**4** I want to try ( draw / drawing ).

**5** The ( act / acting ) lessons start at five o'clock.

**6** My favourite hobby is ( skateboard / skateboarding ).

**3** **Write the verbs in the correct form.**

I'm good at _____ (sing karaoke) but I'm not very good at _____ (act).

He is good at _____ (play chess) but he isn't very good at _____ (play football).

We're good at _____ (trampoline) but we aren't good at _____ (draw).

# Unit 4

**1** Think and complete the words. Then draw.

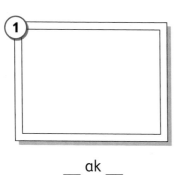

__ ak __

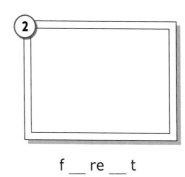

f __ re __ t

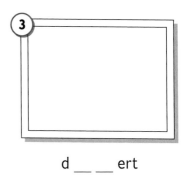

d __ __ ert

**2** Complete the questions with the plural form of the words. Then write the answers.

> volcano   pyramid   statue   lake   city

**1** How many ___volcanoes___ are there in your country? _____

**2** How many _____ are there in your country? _____

**3** How many _____ are there in your country? _____

**4** How many _____ are there in your country? _____

**5** How many _____ are there in your country? _____

**3** Put the words in order to write questions and sentences.

**1** is / there / a big forest / China / in / ?

Is there a big forest in China?

**2** a city / on a volcano / in Japan / there's / .

_____

**3** United Kingdom / the / in / there / are / lots of / statues / .

_____

**4** any / pyramids / are / in / Spain / there / ?

_____

# Unit 5

**(1) Match the words with the definitions.**

| | | | | |
|---|---|---|---|---|
| **1** | swimsuit | **a** | you put money in this |
| **2** | watch | **b** | this keeps you dry |
| **3** | wallet | **c** | you wear this at the beach |
| **4** | umbrella | **d** | you wear this at the gym |
| **5** | belt | **e** | this tells you the time |
| **6** | tracksuit | **f** | you wear this with your jeans |

**(2) Complete the sentences with the correct form of the verb + *going to*.**

Look! I ¹_____ (buy) that bracelet for my mum's birthday! It's so beautiful.

I want to buy a new swimsuit for myself but I haven't got enough money.

We ²_____ (save) money this spring.

³_____ they ⁴_____ (go shopping) today or tomorrow?

**(3) Complete the sentences.**

**1** This watch is _____. It is my watch.

**2** This belt is _____. It is your belt.

**3** These gloves are _____. They are his gloves.

**4** This bracelet is _____. It is her bracelet.

**5** These umbrellas are _____. They are our umbrellas.

**6** These tracksuits are _____. They are their tracksuits.

# Unit 6

**(1) Read and find the mistakes. Then write the verb in the correct form.**

It was my birthday yesterday. I haved a big party. My mum make a cake and some sandwiches. My friends comed and bring me a lot of presents. We danced and singed. We played games and had a great time.

1 _____  2 _____  3 _____

4 _____  5 _____

**(2) Read the answers and write the questions.**

1 _____? I went to Mexico.

3 _____? I saw amazing pyramids!

2 _____? I travelled in July.

4 _____? I met some kind and interesting people.

**(3) What did you do yesterday? Write sentences.**

> tidy my room   make a cake   do my homework
> see friends   revise for a test   take notes in class

Yesterday I did a lot of things. First, I _____

_____

_____

_____

# Unit 7

**1** **Read and complete.**

> exciting   interesting   scary   easy   boring

Yesterday was a really bad day. I was in my History lesson and it was $^1$_____.
Suddenly, I saw a ghost and it was so $^2$_____. I tried to run but it wasn't
$^3$_____. The ghost took all our tests from the desk and threw them in the air. It
was funny and $^4$_____. Then I heard my name, 'John! John! Wake up!' The ghost
was dream – a very $^5$_____ dream!

**2** **Find the mistakes. Then write the correct school subjects.**

**1**   We study numbers in Geography. _____

**2**   We learn about musical instruments in Drama. _____

**3**   Computer Studies teaches you to speak French. _____

**4**   Science helps us learn about different countries. _____

**3** **Look at your timetable. Complete the questions and answer for you.**

> Maths   Geography   Science   History   Art   Music   Sports

**1**   Did you have _____ last Monday?   _____.

**2**   Did you have _____ last Friday morning?   _____.

**3**   Did you have _____ last Wednesday?   _____.

**4**   Did you have _____ last Tuesday?   _____.

# Unit 8

**1** **Read. Then draw and colour the flags.**

**1**

Tess is Australian.

**2**

Omar is Turkish.

**3**

Lia is Spanish.

**4**

Mia is Polish.

**2** **Read. Then write sentences.**

who   that   which   where

**1**   She is a musician. She is also good at acting.

She is a musician who is also good at acting.

**2**   My grandad was born in 1945. It was the year the Second World War ended.

_____

**3**   This is a famous statue. It is from China.

_____

**4**   This is the shopping mall in our town. It is the place I meet my friends.

_____

**3** **Complete the sentences.**

**1**   A photographer is a person _____.

**2**   A restaurant is a place _____.

**3**   My mum is a doctor _____.

**4**   The story is about a village _____.

**5**   This is the car _____.

# Picture Dictionary

## Unit 1 Friends

### Physical appearance

 dark hair

 spiky hair

 handsome

 good-looking

 moustache

 blond(e) hair

 bald

 beautiful

 cute

 beard

 straight hair

 curly hair

### Adjectives to describe personality

 bossy

 kind

 sporty

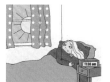 lazy

 clever

 shy

 talkative

 helpful

 friendly

 hard-working

### Art

 abstract

 etching

 expressionism

 detail

 post-impressionism

 sharp

# Unit 2 My life

## Daily activities

brush my teeth

make my bed

wash my face

tidy my room

do my homework

go to bed early

revise for a test

take notes in class

take out the rubbish

be on time

## Adverbs of frequency

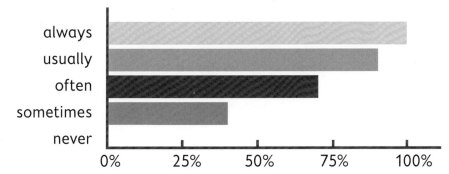

## Your digestion

saliva

nutrients

minerals

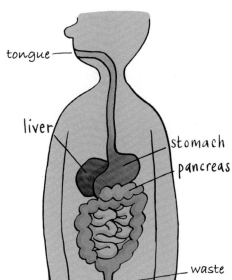

# Unit 3 Free time

## Hobbies and activities

hitting

kicking

throwing

catching

diving

doing puzzles

telling jokes

reading poetry

playing computer games

trampolining

playing chess

playing the drums

acting

rollerblading

running races

singing karaoke

skateboarding

writing stories

drawing

## Apps

apps

download

upload

online

social media

# Unit 4 Around the world

## Countries

China

South Korea

Japan

Australia

the United States

Mexico

Argentina

Brazil

Poland

the United Kingdom

Spain

Italy

Egypt

Turkey

## Places

forest

desert

pyramid

statue

city

cave

volcano

lake

## The solar system

air

gravity

moon

planet

rings

space

# Unit 5 Shopping

## Clothing and accessories

 tracksuit

 swimsuit

 watch

 bracelet

 wallet

 pocket

 belt

 umbrella

 gloves

 label

## Adjectives for clothes

 tight

 baggy

 cheap

 expensive

 old-fashioned

 modern

 too big

 not big enough

 floral

 colourful

## Shopping

 advertisement

 receipt

 change

 money

 customer

 department store

 coupons

# Unit 6 Party time

## Irregular past tense verbs

make/made

have/had

come/came

give/gave

get/got

sing/sang

bring/brought

meet/met

eat/ate

see/saw

## Parties

wedding

tea party

graduation party

dinner party

fancy dress party

surprise party

pyjama party

farewell party

picnic

## The first Thanksgiving

celebrated

crossed

landed

months

Native American

settler

voyage

# Unit 7 School

## Adjectives

interesting

boring

exciting

scary

embarrassing

funny

difficult

easy

romantic

important

## School subjects

Computer Studies

Maths

Geography

Science

History

Art

Music

Sport

Design

Drama

## Flu and germs

coughing

flu

germs

scrub

spread

symptoms

# Unit 8 All about us

## Nationalities

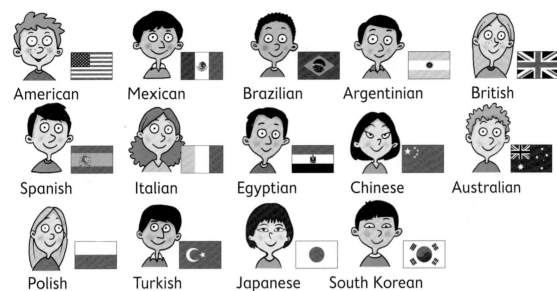

American

Mexican

Brazilian

Argentinian

British

Spanish

Italian

Egyptian

Chinese

Australian

Polish

Turkish

Japanese

South Korean

## Occupations

scientist

sailor

businessman/
businesswoman

musician

waiter

actor

engineer

mechanic

footballer

TV presenter

## Inventions

idea

inventor

invention

create

design

construct

**Pearson Education Limited**
KAO Two
KAO Park
Harlow
Essex CM17 9NA
England
and Associated Companies throughout the world.

Poptropica® English Islands

© Pearson Education Limited 2018

Editorial and project management by hyphen

First published 2018
ISBN: 978-1-292-19871-2

Set in Fiendstar 16/21pt
Printed in Neografia, Slovakia

**Acknowledgements:** The publisher would like to thank Catherine Zgouras, John Wiltshier and José Luis Morales for their contributions to this edition.

**Illustrators:** Charlotte Alder (The Bright Agency), Fred Blunt, Moreno Chiacchiera (Beehive Illustration), Lawrence Christmas, Leo Cultura, Mark Draisey, HL Studios, Sue King (Plum Pudding Illustration), John Martz, Simone Massoni (Advocate Art), Rob McClurkan (Beehive Illustration), Ken Mok, Olimpia Wong, Christos Skaltsas (hyphen)

**Picture Credits**
The publisher would like to thank the following for their kind permission to reproduce their photographs:

(Key: b-bottom; c-centre; l-left; r-right; t-top)

**123RF.com:** 9t, 16cr, 31/1, Carol Lynn Tice 12br, 104 (sharp), Etkai7 106 (upload), Gleb TV 104 (cute), Iconogenic 108 (colourful), Jose Manuel Gelpi Diaz 27cr, Julias art 106 (download), Robert P Mobley Jr 72cr, Vladzoco 41 (Peter), Cathy Yeulet 41 (Sandra); **Alamy Stock Photo:** Allstar Picture Library 76bc, Cultura Creative 109 (surprise party), Design Pics Inc 51tc, Granger Historical Picture Archive 12c/2, 104 (expressionism), Imagebroker 51tl, 81tl, Interfoto 76cl, Juice Images 81tr, Mamunur Rashid 73cr, manwithacamera.com.au 76cr, MBI 51tr, Oxana Oleynichenko 79cr, Spotmatik 31/2, Wenn Ltd 76c, Zuma Press Inc. 76br; Fotolia.com: CandyBox Images 21tl, Promesa Art Studio 78 (Mexico), 107 (Mexico), Simon Kr 104 (beard), Yuri Arcurs 104 (good looking); **Getty Images:** iStock / Ann Worthy 77/4, Echo / Juice Image 77/1, Echo / Juice Images 77/2, Blend Images / Inti St Clair 77/6, Masko 77/5, Mieke Dalle 108 (not big enough), Photodisc 23cr, Rocky Widner 79br, Westend61 108 (too big), Yasuyoshi Chiba 79r; Imagemore Co., Ltd: 78 (Japan), 107 (Japan); Pearson Education Ltd: Studio 8 9tl, 9tr, Jon Barlow 9tc; **Shutterstock.com:** Adwo 33tc, Alena Ozerova 19tr, Armation 72c, Everett - Art 12cl/1, 104 (detail), 104 (etching), 104 (post-impressionism), Avava 41 (Sofia), Baranq 106 (online), Billion Photos 33cr, Ana Bokan 4/4, Brad Sauter 104 (blonde hair), Cagla Acikgoz 105bc, Catalin Petolea 53cr, Chaoss 108 (modern), charnsitr 107 (United States), Christo 18tr, Clivewa 12cr/3, 104 (abstract), Creatista 41 (Diego), demidoff 108, DNF Style 108 (baggy), Colman Lerner Gerardo 37cr, Gladskikh Tatiana 24tr, Globe Turner 107 (South Korea), Halfpoint 109 (wedding), Blend Images 4/1, Monkey Business Images 4/2, Odua Images 4/3, Ioannis Pantzi 104 (dark hair), Iofoto 81cl, Jaimie Duplass 72bl, Jason Stitt 104 (spiky hair), Joca de Jong 41 (Maria), Kakigori Studio 72cl, Kameel4u 21tc, Karkas 108 (floral), Kerdkanno 105bl, Kite Rin 104 (beautiful), Lanych 109 (fancy dress party), Leungchopan 4/6, Lisa F. Young 104 (bald), JHDT Stock Images LLC 4/5, MadamLead 41 (George), Martial Red 106 (social media), Mary Valery 105b, Mavo 104 (curly hair), Maya Kruchankova 109 (pyjama party), Mehmet Dilsiz 27br, New Photo Service 77/3, Nexus 7 108 (expensive), Nikola Bilic 108 (old-fashioned), Olena Yakobchuk 59tr, Olga Klochanko 109 (dinner party), Olillia 109 (celebrated), Oreshcka 64br, Pi-Lens 43c, Piotr Wawrzyniuk 63c, Raksha Shelare 56br, Rawpixel.com 104 (moustache), 109 (farewell party), Sergei Bachlakov 33tr, Sergio Sallovitz 109 (tea party), Serj Malomuzh 43bc, Sonya Etchison 13tr, Steffen Foerster 43cr, Steve Horsley 109 (graduation party), Titelio 108 (cheap), Happy Together 31/3, Tovovan 109 (crossed), Tracy Whiteside 18br, Valua Vitaly 104 (straight hair), Vgstudio 104 (handsome), Victor Brave 72br, Vjom 106 (apps), Wavebreakmedia 109 (picnic), XiXinXing 13cr
All other images © Pearson Education

Every effort has been made to trace the copyright holders and we apologise in advance for any unintentional omissions. We would be pleased to insert the appropriate acknowledgement in any subsequent edition of this publication.